Algebraic Theory of Automata

ACM MONOGRAPH SERIES

*Published under the auspices of the Association for
Computing Machinery Inc.*

Edited by ROBERT L. ASHENHURST   *The University of Chicago*

A. FINERMAN (Ed.)   University Education in Computing Science, 1968
A. GINZBURG   Algebraic Theory of Automata, 1968
E. F. CODD   Cellular Automata, 1968
G. ERNST AND A. NEWELL   GPS: A Case Study in Generality and Problem Solving, 1969
M. A. GAVRILOV AND A. D. ZAKREVSKII   LYaPAS: A Programming Language for Logic and Coding Algorithms, 1969

*Previously published and available from The Macmillan Company,
New York City*
G. SEBESTYN   Decision Making Processes in Pattern Recognition, 1963
M. YOVITS (Ed.)   Large Capacity Memory Techniques for Computing Systems, 1962
V. KRYLOV   Approximate Calculation of Integrals (Translated by A. H. Stroud), 1962

Algebraic Theory of Automata

Abraham Ginzburg

CARNEGIE–MELLON UNIVERSITY
PITTSBURGH, PENNSYLVANIA
THE TECHNION
ISRAEL INSTITUTE OF TECHNOLOGY
HAIFA, ISRAEL

ACADEMIC PRESS   New York · London   1968

ACADEMIC PRESS, INC.
111 Fifth Avenue, New York, New York 10003

United Kingdom Edition published by
ACADEMIC PRESS, INC. (LONDON) LTD.
Berkeley Square House, London W1X6BA

LIBRARY OF CONGRESS CATALOG CARD NUMBER: 68-23497

Second Printing, 1969

PRINTED IN THE UNITED STATES OF AMERICA

Preface

This monograph is intended to provide a graduate student and a newcomer to the field with ideas, methods, and results of algebraic theory of automata; nevertheless, people working in the area may find the book useful, too, especially the chapters about regular expressions and the decomposition theory of Krohn and Rhodes.

The book can serve as a text for a one-semester course in Automata Theory.

The contents of the monograph need not be discussed here (see the Table of Contents) but for the following two remarks:

1. The purpose of Chapter 1 is to enable the reader with a weaker algebraic preparation to study the book without too many detours to an algebra text.
2. The limited scope of the publication and the desire to cover the topics with appropriate depth excluded automatically some aspects of the subject; the choice was largely biased by the author's personal interests.

The relational representation of automata is used in this book. Coupled with several additional techniques it proves to be a very convenient tool to deal with the theory of finite automata. Many results allow shorter and simpler proofs, and new insight is often gained.

The regular expressions are treated by means of transition graphs and tables of derivatives, thus avoiding the usual quite cumbersome algebraic manipulations.

The bibliography contains mainly titles that are referred to directly.

The author is grateful to the ACM and Academic Press for their willingness to include this book in the ACM Monograph Series, and to the Advanced Research Projects Agency of the Office of the Secretary of Defense (SD-146) for supporting this work.

Sincere thanks are due to Mrs. Dorothy Josephson, from the unusually efficient office of the Computer Science Department at Carnegie–Mellon

v

University of Pittsburgh, for her devotion, patience, and skill in typing this sub-superscript material.

Professor David Parnas, Mrs. Carol Thompson, Mr. Zohar Manna, and Dr. Abraham Lempel read parts of the manuscript, and their criticism and remarks are greatly appreciated.

Special thanks are due to Professor Albert R. Meyer for his help in improving the manuscript. Section 7.12 and a large portion of Section 5.6 which were written by him together with his numerous suggestions, comments, and corrections make his contribution to this book extremely valuable.

Finally, the author is greatly indebted to the Computer Science and Mathematics Departments at Carnegie–Mellon University, and especially to the heads of these departments, Professor Alan J. Perlis and Professor Ignace I. Kolodner, for the privilege of doing this work in a most inspiring and generous atmosphere, and for their constant encouragement and assistance.

Pittsburgh, Pennsylvania   ABRAHAM GINZBURG

Contents

Chapter 3. **Recognizers (Rabin–Scott Automata)**

Chapter 4. **Regular Expressions**

Chapter 5. **Coverings of Automata**

Chapter 6. **Covering by Permutation and Reset Semiautomata**

Chapter 7. **The Theory of Krohn and Rhodes**

Chapter 1

Algebraic Preliminaries

Algebraic notions and connections used later are presented in this chapter. Many readers will presumably prefer only to scan it briefly and return when necessary to specific facts and theorems discussed here.

1.1 Sets

The symbol $P \Rightarrow Q$ indicates that P implies Q, i.e., if P is true then Q is true.

The symbol $P \Leftrightarrow Q$ indicates that P implies Q and Q implies P; in words: P if and only if Q.

The notions of a *set* and an *element of a set* are considered as basic and taken without definition.

The following notations are also used:

$\{a \mid P\}$ the set of all such elements a (from some set) which satisfy the property P.

$a \in A$ a is an element of the set A.

$a \notin A$ a is not an element of the set A.

ϕ the *empty* set, i.e., the set which does not contain any elements.

Let A and B be sets. If $a \in A \Rightarrow a \in B$ then A is said to be a *subset* of B, which is denoted by $A \subseteq B$ or $B \supseteq A$. For every set A, $\phi \subseteq A$, $A \subseteq A$.

1

$A = B \Leftrightarrow A \subseteq B$ and $B \subseteq A$.

$A \cup B$ denotes the (set theoretical) *union* of the sets A and B, which is the set of all elements belonging to A or to B, or to both.

$A \cap B$, the *intersection* of A and B, is the set of all elements belonging to A and B simultaneously.

Clearly,

$$A \cup B = A \Leftrightarrow A \cap B = B \Leftrightarrow A \supseteq B.$$

$A - B$ is the set of all elements in A which are not in B.

The set of all ordered pairs (a, b) $(a \in A, b \in B)$ is called the *Cartesian product* of A and B and is denoted by $A \times B$.

Similarly, one defines a Cartesian product of any finite number of sets.

1.2   Relations and Mappings

Any subset of $A \times B$ is called a (*binary*) *relation* between A and B. Let R be a relation between A and B, i.e., R is a set of pairs (a, b), where $a \in A$, $b \in B$. $(a, b) \in R$ is often expressed also in the form $\begin{pmatrix} a \\ b \end{pmatrix} \in R$ or $a \, R \, b$.

The *inverse relation* R^{-1} is defined by

$$b \, R^{-1} \, a \Leftrightarrow a \, R \, b.$$

R^{-1} is a relation between B and A.

Relations between A and A will be mostly considered; they are said to be relations *over* A. If R is a relation over A, so is R^{-1}.

$pr_1 R = \{a \mid \exists \, b, a \, R \, b\}$ is the set of all such a's for which there exists at least one b such that $a \, R \, b$ holds.

$$pr_2 R = pr_1 R^{-1}, \qquad \text{that is} \qquad pr_2 R = \{b \mid \exists \, a, a \, R \, b\}.$$

By definition, $pr_1 R \subseteq A$, $pr_2 R \subseteq B$.

$pr_1 R$ is also called *the domain* of R, $pr_2 R$ is called the *range* of R.

A relation φ satisfying:

$$a \, \varphi \, b_1, a \, \varphi \, b_2 \Rightarrow b_1 = b_2$$

(in words: every element of $pr_1\varphi$ is in relation φ with exactly one element of B) is called a *mapping from A into B*.

In other words, φ is a *mapping* from the set A into the set B if φ "assigns" to every element of some subset of A (called the domain of φ) one and only one element of B.

Distinct elements of A can be, of course, mapped by φ on the same element of B.

If $pr_1\varphi = A$, then φ is a mapping *of A into B*.

If $pr_1\varphi = A$ and $pr_2\varphi = B$, then φ is a mapping *of A onto B*.

A mapping is often also called a *function*. The *image* of a under the mapping φ is denoted by $\varphi(a)$ or $a\varphi$.

For any relation,

$$R(a) = aR = \{b \mid a \, R \, b\}.$$

For $A_1 \subseteq A$,

$$R(A_1) = A_1 R = \bigcup_{a \in A_1} R(a).$$

If φ is a mapping, φ^{-1} need not be. In case it is, φ is called a *one-to-one mapping*. In other words, φ is a one-to-one mapping from A into B if φ is a mapping from A into B, and for any two distinct a_1, a_2 in the domain of ψ: $\varphi(a_1) \neq \varphi(a_2)$. In this case φ^{-1} is a mapping of the range of φ (a subset of B) onto the domain of φ (a subset of A).

The sets A and B are said to have the same *cardinality* if there exists a one-to-one mapping *of A onto B*. In the finite case this means that A and B have the same number of elements. In the infinite case, a proper (i.e., distinct from A) subset of a set A may have the same cardinality as A (e.g., the even integers and all integers). Moreover, this property characterizes infinite sets.

A one-to-one mapping of a set A onto itself is called a *permutation*. If φ is a permutation, then φ^{-1} is, too.

1.3   Groupoids, Semigroups

A set A with a mapping φ from the Cartesian product $A \times A$ into A forms a *partial binary single-valued multiplicative system* (or, briefly, a partial binary system), usually also denoted by A.

In other words, A is a partial binary system if there is defined an *operation* (called, say, multiplication) in A, which "combines" some ordered pairs of elements of A to give, in result, an element of A. One writes instead of $(a_1, a_2)\varphi = a_3$ simply

$$a_1 a_2 = a_3 \qquad (a_1, a_2, a_3 \in A).$$

If the operation is defined for all pairs of $A \times A$ it is called total, and A, with that operation, is called a (complete) *binary system* or *groupoid*.

A finite groupoid can be conveniently described by a "multiplication table" similar to those from elementary arithmetic.

The operation in a groupoid can be subject to certain axioms. In particular, the so-called *associativity* is very often required:

For every $a, b, c \in A$

$$(ab)c = a(bc).$$

An induction proof can be provided to the effect that the above implies that the product of an arbitrary number of elements in A will be independent on the particular arrangement of brackets.

A groupoid fulfilling the axiom of associativity is called an *associative groupoid*, or a *semigroup*. In a semigroup one writes abc without brackets, and can apply the usual power notation: a^n for $aa \ldots a$ (n times) with the familiar laws: $a^n a^m = a^{n+m}$, $(a^n)^m = a^{nm}$.

The positive integers form a semigroup under addition and also under multiplication. The following multiplication tables describe two semigroups, each one consisting of three elements:

	a	b	c
a	a	b	c
b	b	b	c
c	c	b	c

	0	1	2
0	0	1	2
1	1	2	0
2	2	0	1

A semigroup, which is of particular importance in the sequel, will now be described.

Let $\Sigma = \{\sigma_0, \sigma_1, \ldots, \sigma_{m-1}\}$ be a finite set of symbols called, also, *letters*; accordingly, Σ is called an *alphabet*.

A *word* (often called, also, a *string*, or a *tape*) over Σ is a finite sequence of letters from Σ written one after the other without any intermediate signs. (For example, $\sigma_1\sigma_2$, $\sigma_2\sigma_1$, $\sigma_0\sigma_3\sigma_{m-1}\sigma_3\sigma_3$ are words over Σ. Notice that $\sigma_1\sigma_2$ and $\sigma_2\sigma_1$ are distinct words.)

One considers, also, the so-called *empty word*, i.e., the word which does not have any letters; it is denoted by $\wedge$. The *length* of a word is the number of letters in it. The length of $\wedge$ is 0.

Σ^* denotes the set of all words over Σ (including the empty one) with the operation of concatenation of words which combines to one word an ordered pair of words by writing the letters of the second after those of the first. For example,

$$\sigma_1\sigma_3\sigma_3\sigma_2 \cdot \sigma_0\sigma_2\sigma_1 = \sigma_1\sigma_3\sigma_3\sigma_2\sigma_0\sigma_2\sigma_1.$$

For $\wedge$ one has by definition, $w\wedge = \wedge w = w$ for every word w in Σ^*.

Thus, Σ^* is a groupoid; moreover, it is a semigroup, because the above operation is evidently associative. This semigroup is called the *free semigroup* generated by Σ, and the set Σ is called the set of *generators* of Σ^*.

Another important example of a semigroup is provided by the relations over a set A.

Let R and S be two relations over A. The relation T defined as follows:

$$a\,T\,b \Leftrightarrow \exists\, c \quad \text{such that} \quad a\,R\,c \quad \text{and} \quad c\,S\,b$$

is called *the composition* or *the product* of R and S (in this order): $T = RS$.

Notice:

$$RS = \phi \Leftrightarrow pr_2 R \cap pr_1 S = \phi.$$

The composition of relations is associative. Indeed,

$$a\,(RS)T\,b \Leftrightarrow \exists\, x(a\,RS\,x,\ x\,T\,b) \Leftrightarrow \exists\, x\, \exists\, y(a\,R\,y,\ y\,S\,x,\ x\,T\,b)$$

$$\Leftrightarrow \exists\, y(a\,R\,y,\ y\,ST\,b) \Leftrightarrow a\,R(ST)\,b.$$

Thus, the set of all relations over A with the above defined multiplication forms a semigroup.

One can also multiply a relation R between A and B by a relation S between B and C using the same definition:

$$a \; RS \; c \Leftrightarrow \exists \, b(a \; R \; b, \, b \; S \; c).$$

Here $a \in A$, $b \in B$, $c \in C$, and RS is a relation between A and C. Notice:

$$pr_1(RS) \subseteq pr_1 R; \quad pr_2(RS) \subseteq pr_2 S; \quad (RS)^{-1} = S^{-1} R^{-1}.$$

Indeed:

$$c(RS)^{-1} a \Leftrightarrow a \; RS \; c \Leftrightarrow \exists \, b(a \; R \; b, \, b \; S \; c)$$
$$\Leftrightarrow \exists \, b(c \; S^{-1} \; b, \, b \; R^{-1} \; a) \Leftrightarrow c \; S^{-1} R^{-1} \; a.$$

The identity relation I_A over A is the set of all pairs (a, a), $a \in A$. For any relation R over A:

$$RI_A = I_A R = R.$$

The product $\varphi\psi$ of two mappings φ and ψ is easily seen to be a mapping.

Let φ be a mapping of A into B. Then $\varphi\varphi^{-1}$ is a relation over A including I_A, but $\varphi^{-1}\varphi = I_{pr_2\varphi}$. Indeed, $I_{pr_2\varphi}$ is clearly included in $\varphi^{-1}\varphi$ and

$$x\varphi^{-1}\varphi y \Rightarrow \exists \, z(x\varphi^{-1}z, \, z\varphi y) \Rightarrow z\varphi x, \, z\varphi y \Rightarrow x = y$$

because φ is a mapping. If φ is a permutation of A, then $\varphi\varphi^{-1} = \varphi^{-1}\varphi = I_A$.

Let $R_1, R_2, \ldots, R_p$ be relations over a finite set A. Add to them the products of all possible ordered pairs of these relations, then of all possible ordered triples, and so on. Every relation is a subset of $A \times A$. The maximal number of distinct relations over A is $2^{|A|^2}$ where $|A|$ denotes the number of elements of the set A. It follows that at some step of the above computation there will be no more new products, i.e., the products of, say, every ordered n-tuple of relations from the given set equals the product of some m-tuple with $m < n$. Clearly, further multiplication will not add new relations. The so-obtained set of relations over A is closed under multiplication of relations (i.e., the product of any two elements of the set belongs to it) and so it forms a semigroup P of relations. P is said to be *generated* by the relations $R_1, R_2, \ldots, R_p$. The reader should convince himself that any semigroup of relations containing $R_1, \ldots, R_p$ must contain P.

It may happen that P will contain all relations over A, i.e., the semigroup P is actually the semigroup G of all relations over A. But it is also possible that P is properly included in G. P is, in this case, a *subsemigroup* of G.

In general, a subset H of a groupoid G forms a *subgroupoid* of G if H is closed under the operation in G, i.e., if the elements of H form a groupoid when multiplied as in G.

The positive integers form a subsemigroup of the semigroup of all integers under multiplication. The negative integers do not form a subsemigroup of this semigroup, because the product of two negative integers is positive.

In the semigroup

	a	b	c
a	a	b	c
b	b	b	c
c	c	b	c

every subset forms a subsemigroup.

The semigroup

	0	1	2
0	0	1	2
1	1	2	0
2	2	0	1

has only two subsemigroups: the semigroup itself and the set $\{0\}$.

An element e in a groupoid, for which $ee = e$ is called *an idempotent*. An idempotent always forms a subgroupoid.

The set T_A of all mappings of a set A into itself forms a subsemigroup of the semigroup of all relations over A, because, as mentioned, the product of two mappings is a mapping. For a finite A the set T_A has $|A|^{|A|}$ elements.

Any subset of T_A generates a subsemigroup of T_A. These subsemigroups are known as *semigroups of transformations* and play an important role in the theory of semigroups.

The product of two permutations of A is again a permutation of A; hence, the set of all permutations of A (in the finite case it consists of $|A|!$ elements) forms a subsemigroup of T_A, and, of course, also of the semigroup of all relations over A.

1.4   Identity, Monoid

An important axiom, rather seldom assumed in the sequel, is *commutativity*:

For every a, b:

$$ab = ba.$$

Commutativity of a groupoid can be easily checked by inspecting its multiplication table. Indeed, the groupoid is commutative if and only if that table is symmetric with respect to its main diagonal.

There are many known examples of commutative groupoids and semigroups; the integers form a commutative semigroup under addition and also under multiplication.

On the other hand, composition of relations is not commutative. For example,

$$\begin{pmatrix} 1 & 1 & 2 & 3 \\ 2 & 3 & 2 & 1 \end{pmatrix} \begin{pmatrix} 1 & 3 & 3 \\ 3 & 2 & 3 \end{pmatrix} = \begin{pmatrix} 1 & 1 & 3 \\ 2 & 3 & 3 \end{pmatrix}$$

but

$$\begin{pmatrix} 1 & 3 & 3 \\ 3 & 2 & 3 \end{pmatrix} \begin{pmatrix} 1 & 1 & 2 & 3 \\ 2 & 3 & 2 & 1 \end{pmatrix} = \begin{pmatrix} 1 & 3 & 3 \\ 1 & 2 & 1 \end{pmatrix}.$$

Thus, semigroups of relations, semigroups of mappings, and semigroups of permutations are, in general, not commutative.

Some elements of a groupoid may have special properties with respect to the operation, e.g., the idempotency mentioned above.

An element e_l of a groupoid is called a *left* identity if for every a in this groupoid:

$$e_l a = a.$$

As $e_l e_l = e_l$, every left identity is an idempotent (but not vice versa). Similarly, one defines a right identity e_r. Now $e_l e_r = e_r$, but $e_l e_r = e_l$ also, hence, $e_l = e_r$; i.e., if a groupoid has a left identity and a right one, they must coincide. This element—a left and right identity or a two-sided identity—is called (if it exists) *the identity* of the groupoid, and as is clear from the above, a groupoid can have at most one identity.

The semigroup of positive integers under addition does not have an identity, but the semigroups of all integers or all nonnegative integers under addition have identities: the number 0 in both cases.

The free semigroup Σ^* over an alphabet Σ has an identity: the empty word $\wedge$.

The identity relation I_A serves as an identity in the semigroups of all relations over A, all mappings of A, and all permutations of A.

A semigroup with an identity is called *a monoid*. Given a semigroup G without identity, add to G an element e (assume that e is a symbol which does not appear among those denoting the elements of G) and require:

$$ee = e \quad \text{and} \quad eg = ge = g \qquad \text{for every} \quad g \in G.$$

$G \cup \{e\}$ is now a monoid with the identity e. Thus, every semigroup without identity can be augmented to a monoid by adding an identity element.

1.5 Isomorphism. Representation of Monoids by Right Translations

Two groupoids G_1 and G_2 are said to be *isomorphic* (notation: $G_1 \simeq G_2$) if there exists a one-to-one mapping φ of G_1 onto G_2 such that for every $a, b \in G_1$:

$$(ab)\varphi = (a\varphi)(b\varphi).$$

(The product ab is computed in G_1 and $(a\varphi)(b\varphi)$ in G_2.) Such a φ is called an *isomorphism* or an *isomorphic mapping*

As far as the properties of the operations (multiplications) are concerned, isomorphic groupoids are indistinguishable: to every element of one there corresponds one and only one element of the other, and this correspondence is preserved by the operations; i.e., the image of a product of two elements is equal to the product of their images. On the other hand, the elements of isomorphic groupoids can have quite a distinct nature; thus, isomorphic groupoids cannot be seen as identical.

A classical example provide the groupoid of the positive real numbers under multiplication and the groupoid of the real numbers under addition. Consider the mapping which takes a number a from the first groupoid onto the number $\log a$ of the second. This is a one-to-one mapping of the first groupoid onto the second, and, moreover,

$$\log(ab) = \log a + \log b,$$

i.e., the mapping is an isomorphism.

Given an abstract groupoid G_1 (say, by its multiplication table), one is often interested in finding an isomorphic groupoid G_2 the elements of which are some well-known mathematical objects like numbers, matrices, mappings of a given set, etc. Such a G_2 provides a *faithful (isomorphic)* *representation* of G_1 in "convenient terms."

An important example yields the following theorem:

THEOREM.   Every monoid G can be faithfully represented by a semigroup of mappings.

Proof.   Consider the set $K = \{\theta_g\}$ ($g \in G$) of mappings of the set of elements of G defined as follows: $a\theta_g = ag$, $a \in G$. K is a semigroup. Indeed, one has to show only that K is closed under multiplication. Let g_1, g_2 be arbitrary elements of G, let $g_1 g_2 = g_3$, and compute:

For any $a \in G$

$$a(\theta_{g_1}\theta_{g_2}) = (a\theta_{g_1})\theta_{g_2} = (ag_1)\theta_{g_2} = (ag_1)g_2 = a(g_1g_2) = ag_3 = a\theta_{g_3}.$$

Hence

$$\theta_{g_1}\theta_{g_2} = \theta_{g_3}$$

as required. G is isomorphic to K. Indeed, the mapping φ of G onto K defined by $g\varphi = \theta_g$ is one-to-one, because $g_1 \neq g_2$ implies

$$e\theta_{g_1} = eg_1 = g_1 \neq g_2 = eg_2 = e\theta_{g_2},$$

that is,

$$\theta_{g_1} \neq \theta_{g_2} \qquad (e \text{ is the identity of } G).$$

Finally, the above computation also shows that

$$(g_1g_2)\varphi = \theta_{g_1g_2} = \theta_{g_1}\theta_{g_2} = (g_1\varphi)(g_2\varphi),$$

i.e., φ is an isomorphism.

Notice that the fact that G has an identity is crucial, otherwise θ_{g_1} may be equal to θ_{g_2}, even when $g_1 \neq g_2$, i.e., φ is not necessarily a one-to-one mapping. On the other hand, one can easily convert every semi-group into a monoid, so that the result relates to semigroups in general.

The above theorem does not hold for nonassociative groupoids. Repeat the computation:

$$a(\theta_{g_1}\theta_{g_2}) = (a\theta_{g_1})\theta_{g_2} = (ag_1)\theta_{g_2} = (ag_1)g_2$$

and this is, in general, not equal to

$$a(g_1g_2) = a\theta_{g_1g_2}.$$

The mappings θ_g are also called *right translations* of G.

EXAMPLE.   For

$$G = \begin{array}{c|ccc} & a & b & c \\ \hline a & a & b & c \\ b & b & b & c \\ c & c & b & c \end{array}$$

$$\theta_a = \begin{pmatrix} a & b & c \\ a & b & c \end{pmatrix}, \qquad \theta_b = \begin{pmatrix} a & b & c \\ b & b & b \end{pmatrix}, \qquad \theta_c = \begin{pmatrix} a & b & c \\ c & c & c \end{pmatrix}.$$

1.6   Groups

Let G be a groupoid with an identity e. An element a_l is called a *left inverse* of an element a if $a_l a = e$.

A *right inverse* a_r is defined similarly. An element of a groupoid may have more than one left or right inverse.

If a_l and a_r exist in a monoid, they must coincide:

$$a_l = a_l e = a_l(a a_r) = (a_l a)a_r = e a_r = a_r.$$

Such a two-sided inverse is called *an inverse* of the element a and denoted by a^{-1}: $a^{-1}a = aa^{-1} = e$.

Of course, not every element of a monoid must have an inverse. For example, in the free semigroup of words, only $\wedge$ has an inverse—$\wedge$ itself. It is clear that no other word can be concatenated to give the empty word.

For a relation R over A, the product RR^{-1} is, in general, not equal to the identity relation I_A. But for every permutation P one has $PP^{-1} = P^{-1}P = I_A$. Hence, in the semigroup of all permutations of a set A, every element has an inverse.

A *monoid* in which every element has an inverse is called a *group*.

The integers form a group under addition: zero is the identity and the inverse of a is $-a$.

The positive rational numbers form a group under multiplication: 1 is the identity and $a^{-1} = 1/a$.

The following is a group of three elements:

$$
\begin{array}{c|ccc}
 & 0 & 1 & 2 \\
\hline
0 & 0 & 1 & 2 \\
1 & 1 & 2 & 0 \\
2 & 2 & 0 & 1 \\
\end{array}
$$

0 is the identity, $1^{-1} = 2$, $2^{-1} = 1$. In a group

$$(a^{-1})^{-1} = a, \qquad e^{-1} = e, \qquad (ab)^{-1} = b^{-1}a^{-1}.$$

Denote $a^0 = e$, $a^{-n} = (a^{-1})^n$, and show, easily, that the usual laws of operations with positive and negative exponents hold in a group.

A groupoid (and also a semigroup) can have only one identity, but many idempotents. A group has a unique idempotent—its identity. Indeed,

$$aa = a \Rightarrow a^{-1}aa = a^{-1}a \Rightarrow ea = e \Rightarrow a = e.$$

Every group is a monoid, and the theorem from 1.5 applies likewise to a group. The right translations are, in this case, permutations:

$$a\theta_g = b\theta_g \Rightarrow ag = bg \Rightarrow agg^{-1} = bgg^{-1} \Rightarrow a = b.$$

Hence, every group G can be faithfully represented by a group of permutations of the set of elements of G.

Notice, in a group $ag - bg \Rightarrow a = b$, and, likewise, $ga - gb \Rightarrow a = b$. These are the right and left cancellation laws.

1.7   Reflexivity, Symmetry, Transitivity

Basic properties of groups and semigroups will be discussed in later sections, but first some additional notions from the calculus of relations are needed.

It is assumed, if nothing is said to the contrary, that all relations are over a given set A.

A binary relation R satisfying the condition $I_A \subseteq R$ is called a *reflexive* relation.

If R is reflexive, then R^{-1} is reflexive, $RS \supseteq S$ for any S, $I_A \subseteq R \subseteq R^2 \subseteq \cdots \subseteq R^n \subseteq \cdots$, and if S is also reflexive, then RS is reflexive too.

A relation R is called *symmetric* if $R = R^{-1}$. R^{-1} is symmetric if R is, but the symmetry of R_1 and R_2 does not imply that $R_1 R_2$ is symmetric. For example,

$$R_1 = \begin{pmatrix} a & b \\ b & a \end{pmatrix}, \qquad R_2 = \begin{pmatrix} b & c \\ c & b \end{pmatrix}$$

are symmetric, but

$$R_1 R_2 = \begin{pmatrix} a \\ c \end{pmatrix}$$

is not.

A relation R is called *transitive* if

$$a \, R \, b, \; b \, R \, c \Rightarrow a \, R \, c.$$

An equivalent definition of transitivity is given by the requirement $R^2 \subseteq R$. It follows that a transitive relation fulfills

$$R \supseteq R^2 \supseteq R^3 \supseteq \cdots \supseteq R^n \supseteq \cdots.$$

If R is transitive, so is R^{-1}, but the product of two transitive relations need not be transitive.

EXAMPLE

$$R_1 = \begin{pmatrix} a & c \\ b & d \end{pmatrix}, \qquad R_2 = \begin{pmatrix} b & d \\ c & e \end{pmatrix}, \qquad R_1 R_2 = \begin{pmatrix} a & c \\ c & e \end{pmatrix}.$$

The union

$$\bar{R} = R \cup R^2 \cup R^3 \cup \cdots \cup R^n \cup \cdots$$

is called the *transitive closure* of R. Notice that if R is transitive, then $\bar{R} = R$. In any case, $\bar{R}$ is the smallest transitive relation, including R. Indeed, $a \bar{R} b$, $b \bar{R} c$ implies that for some i and j, $a R^i b$ and $b R^j c$, respectively. But then $a R^{i+j} c$, and, consequently, $a \bar{R} c$. Thus, $\bar{R}$ is transitive. Let S be transitive and include R. Then

$$R \subseteq S \Rightarrow R^2 \subseteq S^2 \subseteq S,$$

i.e., S must include R^2, and in the same way R^3, etc. Hence, $\bar{R} \subseteq S$, and $\bar{R}$ is the smallest transitive relation including R.

Assume that R is reflexive and $|A| = n$. Then $R^2 \supseteq R$, $R^3 \supseteq R^2$, etc. If $R^{i+1} = R^i$ for some i, then all higher powers of R are equal to R^i and $\bar{R} = R^i$. This will actually happen with some $i \leq n - 1$. To prove this, assume $a R^n b$. It means that there exist $c_1, c_2, \ldots, c_{n-1} \in A$ such that

$$a R c_1, c_1 R c_2, \ldots, c_{n-1} R b.$$

But $a, c_1, \ldots, c_{n-1}, b$ are, altogether, $n + 1$ elements of A; hence, at least two of them must be equal, say, $c_j = c_{j+k}$. This implies that $a R^{n-k} b$. (The same will happen if one of the equal elements is a or b.) Therefore, $a R^{n-1} b$ and $R^n \subseteq R^{n-1}$. But $R^n \supseteq R^{n-1}$; hence, $R^n = R^{n-1}$. To summarize: For a reflexive relation R over a finite set A with $|A| = n$, the transitive closure $\bar{R} = R^{n-1}$.

Notice that although a smaller power of R will often do, it is easy to find examples such that R^{n-2} is properly included in R^{n-1}.

1.8 Equivalence Relations, Partitions

A relation which is reflexive, symmetric, and transitive is called an *equivalence relation*.

This is a very important and common kind of relation. For example, equality, parallelness of straight lines or of planes, similarity of triangles, similarity of matrices are equivalence relations.

Let R be an equivalence relation over A. Assume $c \in R(a) \cap R(b)$. Then $a \mathrel{R} c$, $b \mathrel{R} c$, and by symmetry $c \mathrel{R} b$, i.e., $a \mathrel{R} b$ (by transitivity) also. If $x \in R(b)$, i.e., $b \mathrel{R} x$, one obtains by transitivity $a \mathrel{R} x$; hence, $x \in R(a)$; thus, $R(b) \subseteq R(a)$. By symmetry $R(a) \subseteq R(b)$, i.e., $R(a) = R(b)$.

Consider now the subsets $R(a)$, $R(b)$, ... of A. Every element of A belongs to one of them, because R is reflexive. Hence, their union is A. As was shown above, if two such subsets have an element in common, they coincide. Denote the distinct subsets from $R(a)$, $R(b)$, ... by H_1, H_2, ... They are pairwise disjoint, i.e., $H_i \cap H_j = \phi$ and their union is A. This situation is described by saying that the above subsets constitute a *partition* π of A, and each one of the H_i's is called an *equivalence class of R* or a *partition block of π*.

Conversely, let $\pi = \{H_1, H_2, \ldots\}$ be a partition of A, i.e., a set of subsets of A such that they are pairwise disjoint and their union is A.

Define $a \mathrel{R} b \Leftrightarrow a$, b belong to the same block. R is clearly reflexive, symmetric, and transitive; i.e., R is an equivalence relation. Hence, the following theorem:

THEOREM.   Every equivalence relation R over A induces a partition π of A such that a, b belong to the same block of π if and only if $a \mathrel{R} b$; conversely, every partition π of A defines an equivalence relation R over A such that $a \mathrel{R} b$ if and only if a and b belong to the same partition block of π.

EXAMPLE.   Let $A = \{1, 2, 3, 4, 5, 6\}$ and let $\pi = \{\{1, 2, 5\}, \{3\}, \{4, 6\}\}$. The corresponding equivalence relation R is:

$$R = \begin{pmatrix} 1 & 1 & 1 & 2 & 2 & 2 & 5 & 5 & 5 & 3 & 4 & 4 & 6 & 6 \\ 1 & 2 & 5 & 1 & 2 & 5 & 1 & 2 & 5 & 3 & 4 & 6 & 4 & 6 \end{pmatrix}.$$

Conversely, let

$$R = \begin{pmatrix} 1 & 1 & 1 & 1 & 3 & 3 & 3 & 3 & 4 & 4 & 4 & 4 & 5 & 5 & 5 & 5 & 2 & 2 & 6 & 6 \\ 1 & 3 & 4 & 5 & 1 & 3 & 4 & 5 & 1 & 3 & 4 & 5 & 1 & 3 & 4 & 5 & 2 & 6 & 2 & 6 \end{pmatrix}.$$

It can be easily checked that R is reflexive, symmetric and transitive ($R^2 = R$ proves the last assertion). Hence, R is an equivalence. The corresponding partition $\pi = \{\{1, 3, 4, 5\}, \{2, 6\}\}$.

The set of blocks of the partition π corresponding to the equivalence relation R is also called the *quotient set* A/R (or A/π). The number of equivalence classes of R is called the *index* of R. If A/R has a finite number of blocks, R is said to be of *a finite index*.

1.9   Properties of Partitions

The theorem from Section 1.8 establishes a one-to-one correspondence between the equivalence relations over A and the partitions of A. This allows one to deal with partitions using the language of relations and with equivalence relations using the intuitively transparent notion of a partition. All depends on what is more convenient in the given context. There exists a quite elaborated *algebra of partitions*, but here will be mentioned only very basic facts, needed in later discussions.

Let φ be a mapping of A into B. Then $R = \varphi\varphi^{-1}$ is an equivalence relation over A. Indeed, the identity I_A over A is included in R.

$$R^{-1} = (\varphi\varphi^{-1})^{-1} = (\varphi^{-1})^{-1}\varphi^{-1} = \varphi\varphi^{-1} = R$$

and, finally, notice that

$$\varphi^{-1}\varphi = I_{pr_2\varphi} \subseteq I_B$$

hence,

$$R^2 = \varphi\varphi^{-1}\varphi\varphi^{-1} \subseteq \varphi I_B \varphi^{-1} \subseteq \varphi\varphi^{-1} = R.$$

The reader should convince himself that the equivalence classes of R are the subsets of A composed of elements having the same image in B. Actually, starting from this partition of A, it is very easy to see that $\varphi\varphi^{-1}$ is the corresponding equivalence relation which is said to be naturally induced by φ.

Let π be a partition of A. Denote $a \, \pi \, b$ if and only if a and b belong to the same block of π. (In other words if and only if $a \, R \, b$, where R is the equivalence relation over A corresponding to π.)

Now let $\pi_1 = \{H_1, H_2, \ldots\}$ and $\pi_2 = \{K_1, K_2, \ldots\}$ be two partitions of A. Consider the set of nonempty subsets of A obtained by intersecting pairwise the blocks of π_1 with those of π_2, i.e., the nonempty sets among $H_1 \cap K_1$, $H_1 \cap K_2$, $H_2 \cap K_1$, $H_2 \cap K_2$, $\ldots$. As every element of A belongs exactly to one H_i and one K_j, the nonempty intersections form a partition of A. It will be denoted by $\pi_1 \pi_2$ (the *intersection* or the *product* of π_1 and π_2) and is characterized by $a \, \pi_1 \pi_2 \, b \Leftrightarrow a \, \pi_1 \, b$ and $a \, \pi_2 \, b$. The reader is advised to perform the parallel construction in the language of equivalence relations; first prove that $R_1 \cap R_2$ is an equivalence relation if R_1 and R_2 are, and then that the partition $\pi_1 \pi_2$ corresponds to the equivalence relation $R_1 \cap R_2$.

$\pi_1 \leq \pi_2$ (π_1 is finer than π_2) if and only if

$$a \, \pi_1 \, b \Rightarrow a \, \pi_2 \, b,$$

i.e., if and only if every block of π_1 is contained in a block of π_2.

So, clearly,

$$\pi_1 \pi_2 \leq \pi_1 \quad \text{and} \quad \pi_1 \pi_2 \leq \pi_2.$$

The following two partitions are called *trivial*: the partition π_0 in which all elements of A form one block (the corresponding equivalence relation is $A \times A$), and the partition π_{iden} in which every block is a singleton (the corresponding equivalence relation is I_A).

Every π is finer than π_0, and π_{iden} is finer than any π.

1.10   Congruences, Admissible Partitions

An equivalence relation E_r (E_l) over a groupoid G is called a *right* (*left*) *congruence* if $a \, E_r \, b \Rightarrow ax \, E_r \, bx$ ($a \, E_l \, b \Rightarrow xa \, E_l \, xb$, respectively) for every $x \in G$.

An equivalence relation E over G which is both a right and a left congruence is called a *congruence* over G.

In a commutative groupoid every right congruence is a left one; i.e., it is a congruence. This is, in general, not the case in a noncommutative groupoid.

Assuming E is a congruence, one obtains:

$$a \ E \ b, \ c \ E \ d \ \Rightarrow \ ac \ E \ bc, \ bc \ E \ bd \ \Rightarrow \ ac \ E \ bd$$

(because E is transitive). This has a very clear and important interpretation: for any two (distinct or equal) equivalence classes (also called *congruence classes*) H_1 and H_2 of E, the product of any element of H_1 by any element of H_2 will belong to the same equivalence class of E independent of the particular elements chosen. In other words, the partition π corresponding to the congruence E (E is an equivalence) has the property that for any two distinct or equal blocks H_1, H_2 of π there exists a unique block H_3 such that

$$H_1 H_2 \subseteq H_3,$$

where

$$H_1 H_2 = \{ab \mid a \in H_1, b \in H_2\}.$$

Such a partition of a groupoid is called an *admissible partition* (also a partition with the *substitution property*).

Thus, every congruence relation over a groupoid induces an admissible partition of it. It is evident that, conversely, every admissible partition of a groupoid determines in a natural way a congruence relation over it.

For a right congruence relation E_r and the corresponding partition $\pi = \{H_1, H_2, \ldots\}$ one obtains: if a, $b \in H_i$ then for any $x \in G$ there exists an H_k such that $ax, bx \in H_k$; i.e., $H_i x \subseteq H_k$. But, unlike in the congruence case, it is possible that for $x, y \in H_j$, $H_i x$ and $H_i y$ are included in distinct blocks of π.

There follow some examples.

(1)   Consider the group S_3:

	e	a	a^2	b	c	d
e	e	a	a^2	b	c	d
a	a	a^2	e	c	d	b
a^2	a^2	e	a	d	b	c
b	b	d	c	e	a^2	a
c	c	b	d	a	e	a^2
d	d	c	b	a^2	a	e

(S_3 is the group of all permutations of three elements.)

The partition $\pi = \{H_1 = \{e, a, a^2\}, H_2 = \{b, c, d\}\}$ is an admissible one, as can be easily checked. Indeed:

$$H_1H_1 \subseteq H_1, \qquad H_1H_2 \subseteq H_2, \qquad H_2H_1 \subseteq H_2, \qquad H_2H_2 \subseteq H_1.$$

Notice that the inclusions are here actually equalities. The corresponding congruence relation is

$$E = \begin{pmatrix} e & e & e & a & a & a & a^2 & a^2 & a^2 & b & b & b & c & c & c & d & d & d \\ e & a & a^2 & e & a & a^2 & e & a & a^2 & b & c & d & b & c & d & b & c & d \end{pmatrix}.$$

On the other hand, the partition

$$\pi = \{H_1 = \{e, b\}, H_2 = \{a, d\}, H_3 = \{a^2, c\}\}$$

is not admissible, because, for example, the product

$$H_2H_3 = \{aa^2 = e, ac = d, da^2 = b, dc = a\}$$

is not included in any block of π. Thus, the corresponding equivalence is not a congruence. It is a right congruence because

$$H_1e \subseteq H_1, \qquad H_1b \subseteq H_1, \qquad H_1a \subseteq H_2, \qquad H_1d \subseteq H_2,$$

$$H_1a^2 \subseteq H_3, \qquad H_1c \subseteq H_3, \qquad H_2e \subseteq H_2, \qquad H_2b \subseteq H_3$$

(notice, $e, b \in H_1$, but $H_2 e$ and $H_2 b$ belong to distinct blocks of π), $H_2 a \subseteq H_3$, etc.

The equivalence R corresponding to the partition

$$\pi = \{H_1 = \{e, a, b\}, H_2 = \{a^2, c, d\}\}$$

does not have any of the "congruence properties": $H_1 a = \{a, a^2, d\}$ is not a subset of any block, hence, R is not a right congruence; the product $aH_1 = \{a, a^2, c\}$ shows that R is not a left one either.

(2)   Consider the free semigroup Σ^* and define in it the following partition: $H_0 = \{\wedge\}$, $H_1 = \Sigma$ (i.e., all words of length 1), $H_2 = \Sigma^2$ (all words of length 2), etc. This partition is admissible because $\Sigma^i \Sigma^j = \Sigma^{i+j}$ for any i and j (the product of any word of length i by a word of length j is always a word of length $i + j$). The number of congruence classes (i.e., the index of the corresponding congruence) is here infinite.

Another admissible partition of Σ^* can be obtained as follows: every word of length n or less forms a separate partition block; all words longer than n form one partition block. The reader will convince himself easily that this is indeed an admissible partition of Σ^*. Notice that the index of the congruence is here finite.

(3)   The groupoid in this example is the semigroup of the nonnegative integers under addition. One defines $m \, E \, n \Leftrightarrow p \,|\, m - n$ (in words, the integer p divides without remainder the difference $m - n$). E is an equivalence:

$$p \,|\, m - m, \qquad p \,|\, m - n \Leftrightarrow p \,|\, n - m$$

and

$$p \,|\, m - n, \, p \,|\, n - k \Rightarrow p \,|\, (m - n) + (n - k) = m - k.$$

Now,

$$p \,|\, m - n \Rightarrow p \,|\, (m - n)k = mk - nk$$

and

$$p \mid km - kn,$$

that is,

$$m \, E \, n \Rightarrow mk \, E \, nk \quad \text{and} \quad km \, E \, kn \qquad \text{for every} \quad k.$$

Hence, E is a congruence. The blocks of the corresponding partition consist of the integers leaving the remainder zero when divided by p, those which leave the remainder 1 when divided by $p, \ldots$, those which leave the remainder $p - 1$ when divided by p. Altogether, there are p blocks. They are also called *congruence classes modulo* p; $m \equiv n(\text{mod } p)$ denotes that m and n belong to the same class. For example, if $p = 5$, one obtains the following blocks:

$$0 = \{0, 5, 10, 15, \ldots\}$$
$$1 = \{1, 6, 11, 16, \ldots\}$$
$$2 = \{2, 7, 12, 17, \ldots\}$$
$$3 = \{3, 8, 13, 18, \ldots\}$$
$$4 = \{4, 9, 14, 19, \ldots\}.$$

The admissible partitions of a groupoid G form a subset of the set of all partitions of G. The intersection $\pi_1 \pi_2$ of two admissible partitions π_1 and π_2 is thus a partition of G, but, moreover, if it is an admissible partition.
Indeed,

$$a \, \pi_1 \pi_2 \, b \Leftrightarrow a \, \pi_1 \, b, a \, \pi_2 \, b.$$

Now, for any x:

$$a \, \pi_1 \, b, a \, \pi_2 \, b \Rightarrow ax \, \pi_1 \, bx, ax \, \pi_2 \, bx,$$

hence,

$$ax \, \pi_1 \pi_2 \, bx$$

and similarly

$$xa \; \pi_1\pi_2 \; xb.$$

This proves that $\pi_1\pi_2$ is an admissible partition of G.

1.11 Homomorphism

An admissible partition $\pi = \{H_1, H_2, \ldots\}$ of a groupoid G leads in a natural way to a new groupoid. Consider the set $\{\overline{H}_1, \overline{H}_2, \ldots\}$ and define

$$\overline{H}_i\overline{H}_j = \overline{H}_k \Leftrightarrow H_iH_j \subseteq H_k.$$

The product $\overline{H}_i\overline{H}_j$ can be determined also as follows: one takes an arbitrary element (a representative) from H_i, a representative from H_j, multiplies them (in G, of course), and finds the block H_k to which this product belongs (H_k does not depend on the choice of the representatives). Then $\overline{H}_i\overline{H}_j$ is equal to $\overline{H}_k$. The groupoid $\{\overline{H}_1, \overline{H}_2, \ldots\}$ is called *the factor groupoid* of G over π (or over the corresponding congruence E) and is denoted by G/π (or G/E).

Thus, for the first partition in Example (1) in 1.10 one has the following factor groupoid:

	$\overline{H}_1$	$\overline{H}_2$
$\overline{H}_1$	$\overline{H}_1$	$\overline{H}_2$
$\overline{H}_2$	$\overline{H}_2$	$\overline{H}_1$

In Example (3) one has:

	$\bar{0}$	$\bar{1}$	$\bar{2}$	$\bar{3}$	$\bar{4}$
$\bar{0}$	$\bar{0}$	$\bar{1}$	$\bar{2}$	$\bar{3}$	$\bar{4}$
$\bar{1}$	$\bar{1}$	$\bar{2}$	$\bar{3}$	$\bar{4}$	$\bar{0}$
$\bar{2}$	$\bar{2}$	$\bar{3}$	$\bar{4}$	$\bar{0}$	$\bar{1}$
$\bar{3}$	$\bar{3}$	$\bar{4}$	$\bar{0}$	$\bar{1}$	$\bar{2}$
$\bar{4}$	$\bar{4}$	$\bar{0}$	$\bar{1}$	$\bar{2}$	$\bar{3}$

Let φ be the mapping of G onto G/π defined in the natural way:

$$a\varphi = \bar{H} \Leftrightarrow a \in H,$$

i.e., every element of G is mapped onto the block ("with the bar") to which it belongs. By the definition of the multiplication in G/π one obtains:

$$(a\varphi)(b\varphi) = (ab)\varphi,$$

i.e., φ satisfies the property of the isomorphism except for the fact that the mapping φ is not necessarily one-to-one.

A mapping φ of one groupoid G onto another G', satisfying the property

$$(g_1 g_2)\varphi = (g_1\varphi)(g_2\varphi)$$

multiplication   multiplication
in G in G'

is called a *homomorphic mapping* or a *homomorphism* of G onto G'; G' is called a *homomorphic image* of G.
Notice that an isomorphism is a particular case of a homomorphism. The above can now be reformulated in the following way:

A congruence E over G leads to a factor groupoid G/E, which is a homomorphic image of G under the so-called *natural homomorphism* which maps every element of G onto its congruence class.

The following so-called *Homomorphism theorem* deals with the above notions from the opposite side.

THEOREM.   Let φ be a homomorphism of a groupoid G onto a groupoid G'. $E = \varphi\varphi^{-1}$ is a congruence on G and there exists an isomorphism θ of G/E onto G' such that $\varphi = \psi\theta$, where ψ is the natural homomorphism of G onto G/E.

Proof. E is an equivalence as shown in Section 1.9.

$$a\ E\ b \Rightarrow a\varphi = b\varphi \Rightarrow (a\varphi)(c\varphi) = (b\varphi)(c\varphi)$$
$$\Rightarrow (ac)\varphi = (bc)\varphi \Rightarrow ac\ E\ bc \qquad \text{for any}\quad c\quad\text{in}\quad G;$$

and similarly, $ca\ E\ cb$. Hence, E is a congruence. Let H be a congruence class of E and a an arbitrary element in H. Define $\bar{H}\theta = a\varphi$. θ is a mapping of G/E onto G' ($\bar{H}\theta$ does not depend on the representative because $a, b \in H \Rightarrow a\ E\ b \Rightarrow a\varphi = b\varphi$; θ is onto, because any element of G' is an image under φ of some element of G).
   θ is a homomorphism:

$$(\bar{H}_1\bar{H}_2)\theta = (a_1a_2)\varphi = (a_1\varphi)(a_2\varphi) = (\bar{H}_1\theta)(\bar{H}_2\theta).$$

(Here $a_1 \in H_1$, $a_2 \in H_2$, and $a_1a_2 \in H_3$, where $\bar{H}_3 = \bar{H}_1\bar{H}_2$.)
   θ is one-to-one:

$$H_1\theta = \bar{H}_2\theta \Rightarrow a_1\varphi = a_2\varphi \Rightarrow a_1\ E\ a_2 \Rightarrow H_1 = H_2 \Rightarrow \bar{H}_1 - \bar{H}_2.$$

Thus, θ is an isomorphism of G/E onto G'.
   Now, let $a \in G$ belong to the congruence class H:

$$a\varphi = \bar{H}\theta = (a\psi)\theta = a(\psi\theta), \qquad \text{that is}\quad \varphi = \psi\theta.$$

To summarize: Every congruence relation, i.e., admissible partition of a groupoid G leads to a homomorphic image of G—the factor groupoid G/E; conversely, every homomorphism of G induces an admissible partition of G and the corresponding factor groupoid is isomorphic to the given homomorphic image of G.
   Assume that two congruences E_1 and E_2 are given over a groupoid G and $E_1 \subseteq E_2$. In other words, there are two admissible partitions $\pi_1 = \{H_1, H_2, \ldots\}$ and $\pi_2 = \{K_1, K_2, \ldots\}$ of G, and $\pi_1 \leq \pi_2$, i.e., every block of π_1 is included in some block of π_2. Then G/π_2 is a homomorphic image of G/π_1. Indeed, define

$$\bar{H}_i\varphi = \bar{K}_j \Leftrightarrow H_i \subseteq K_j.$$

φ is a mapping of G/π_1 onto G/π_2 (every H_i is contained in one and only one K_j and every K_j contains some H_i). Now,

$$\overline{H}_1\overline{H}_2 = \overline{H}_3 \Rightarrow H_1H_2 \subseteq H_3 \Rightarrow K_1K_2 \cap K_3 \neq \phi,$$

where $H_1 \subseteq K_1$, $H_2 \subseteq K_2$, and $H_3 \subseteq K_3 \Rightarrow K_1K_2 \subseteq K_3$, because π_2 is an admissible partition $\Rightarrow \overline{K}_1\overline{K}_2 = \overline{K}_3$; hence,

$$(\overline{H}_1\overline{H}_2)\varphi = \overline{H}_3\varphi = \overline{K}_3 = \overline{K}_1\overline{K}_2 = (\overline{H}_1\varphi)(\overline{H}_2\varphi).$$

Thus, φ is a homomorphism.

The partition of G/π_1 induced by φ divides the blocks of π_1 into sets of blocks, each such set corresponding to one block of π_2. This is illustrated in the following figure:

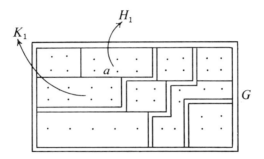

The points are elements of G, the single and double lines define the blocks of π_1, and the double lines those of π_2. The element a belongs to the block H_1 of π_1, and together with this block (and two others) it belongs to the block K_1 of π_2.

The homomorphism φ of G/π_1 onto G/π_2 (when $\pi_1 \leq \pi_2$) is called the *induced homomorphism*.

1.12   Homomorphisms of Semigroups

A homomorphic image of a semigroup is a semigroup. Indeed,

$$(a\varphi b\varphi)c\varphi = (ab)\varphi c\varphi = [(ab)c]\varphi = [a(bc)]\varphi = a\varphi(bc)\varphi = a\varphi(b\varphi c\varphi).$$

A homomorphic image of a monoid is a monoid. To this end, notice that

$$(e\varphi)(a\varphi) = (ea)\varphi = a\varphi, \ (a\varphi)(e\varphi) = (ae)\varphi = a\varphi,$$

i.e., the image of the identity is an identity. Now,

$$(a\varphi)(a^{-1}\varphi) = (aa^{-1})\varphi = e\varphi \text{ and } (a^{-1}\varphi)(a\varphi) = (a^{-1}a)\varphi = e\varphi \Rightarrow$$
$$a^{-1}\varphi = (a\varphi)^{-1},$$

and it follows that a homomorphic image of a group is a group.

A semigroup may have homomorphic images which are groups. This is even true for every groupoid. Let $e \ \overline{|\ e}^{\ e}$ be the groupoid consisting of one element. It is trivially a group. Now, every groupoid G can be mapped homomorphically onto this group by letting all elements of G have e as their image.

A less trivial example was encountered before. For any number p consider the admissible partition π into congruence classes mod p of the monoid Z of the nonnegative integers under addition. The factor semigroup Z/π is a finite monoid of p elements. It is even a group, because every element $\bar{k}$ $(0 < k < p)$ has an inverse: the element $\overline{p - k}$ $(k + p - k = p$ and $p \ \pi \ 0)$. The inverse of $\bar{0}$ is $\bar{0}$. This group is commutative and has a very special property: it can be generated by one element, e.g., by $\bar{1}$. Indeed, $\bar{1} \cdot \bar{1} = \bar{2}$ (because $1 + 1 = 2$), $\bar{2} \cdot \bar{1} = \bar{3}$ $(2 + 1 = 3), \ldots, \overline{p - 2} \cdot \bar{1} = \overline{p - 1}, \ \overline{p - 1} \cdot \bar{1} = \bar{0}$. In other words, every element of this group is a power of $\bar{1}$. (Notice that the operation in Z/π is called multiplication.)

A group which can be generated by one element is called a *cyclic group*. A cyclic group is commutative.

The number of elements of a finite group is called its *order*. Let a be a generator of a cyclic group G of order p. The elements of this group can be written in the form:

$$a, a^2, a^3, \ldots, a^{p-2}, a^{p-1}, a^p = e.$$

The mapping $a^k \varphi = \bar{k}$ is clearly an isomorphism of G onto the group of congruence classes mod p. It follows that up to isomorphism there exists one and only one cyclic group of any finite order p, and each such group can be obtained as a homomorphic image of Z.

An important example of a homomorphism of a semigroup is obtained as follows. Let Σ^* be the free monoid generated by the alphabet $\Sigma = \{\sigma_0, \sigma_1, \ldots, \sigma_{m-1}\}$. ($\Sigma^*$ includes, of course, $\wedge$.) Let $S = \{s_0, s_1, \ldots, s_{n-1}\}$ be a finite set, and let $M = \{I_S, M_{\sigma_0}, M_{\sigma_1}, \ldots, M_{\sigma_{m-1}}\}$ be $m + 1$ mappings, not necessarily all distinct, of S into S (or relations over S). These mappings (relations) generate, as in Section 1.3, a finite semigroup G_A. (*In G_A equal mappings (relations) are represented by one element.*) G_A is a homomorphic image of Σ^*. Indeed, for every word $x = \sigma_{i_1}\sigma_{i_2}\ldots\sigma_{i_j}$ in Σ^* define

$$x\varphi = (\sigma_{i_1}\sigma_{i_2}\ldots\sigma_{i_j})\varphi = M_{\sigma_{i_1}}M_{\sigma_{i_2}}\ldots M_{\sigma_{i_j}} = M_x.$$

The right-hand side expression is a product of mappings (relations) and has to be evaluated in order to obtain the corresponding element of G_A. $\wedge \varphi = I_S$. φ is a mapping of Σ^* onto G_A because every element of G_A is a product of the generators in M, and so it is an image of the corresponding word in Σ^*. For any two words $x = \sigma_{i_1}\sigma_{i_2}\ldots\sigma_{i_j}$, $y = \sigma_{p_1}\sigma_{p_2}\ldots\sigma_{p_q}$ in Σ^*

$$
\begin{aligned}
(xy)\varphi &= M_{\sigma_{i_1}}\ldots M_{\sigma_{i_j}}M_{\sigma_{p_1}}\ldots M_{\sigma_{p_q}} \\
&= (M_{\sigma_{i_1}}\ldots M_{\sigma_{i_j}})(M_{\sigma_{p_1}}\ldots M_{\sigma_{p_q}}) \\
&= (x\varphi)(y\varphi).
\end{aligned}
$$

Hence, φ is a homomorphism.

$E = \varphi\varphi^{-1}$ is a congruence relation over Σ^*. Every congruence class consists of all words x in Σ^* such that the corresponding M_x are the same mappings of S (relations over S). Notice that E has a finite index— the number of elements of G_A.

1.13   Subgroups of a Group

Some notions and results from group theory needed later will be discussed here. It is assumed that the considered groups are finite, although much of what will be said applies equally to infinite groups.

A *subgroup* H of a group G is a subset of G which is itself a group under the operation in G. So, in Example (1) in 1.10, the elements $\{e, a, a^2\}$ form a subgroup of S_3; equally, the elements $\{e, b\}$ and some other subsets. Every group has two trivial subgroups: the group itself and the identity. Any group which is not cyclic has necessarily a nontrivial subgroup. Take any nonidentity element a of this group and consider the cyclic group H generated by it in G. Compute $a, a^2, \ldots, a^i$, $\ldots, a^j, \ldots$. As G is finite, there must be i and j $(i < j)$ such that $a^i = a^j$. Let j be the smallest power of a equal to a previous power of a. Then

$$a^{-i}a^i = a^{-i}a^j,$$

i.e., $e = a^{j-i}$ and $a = a^{j-i+1}$, i.e., $i = 1$ $(j - i + 1 = j$ because j is the smallest power of a equal to a previous one). All elements $a, a^2, \ldots$, $a^{j-1} = e$ are distinct and form the above-mentioned cyclic group generated by a in G. This group is a subgroup of G and it cannot be G itself, because by assumption G is noncyclic. It is left to the reader as a simple exercise to show that a cyclic group of composite order has, and one of prime order has not, nontrivial subgroups.

For any group G, and any element $g \in G$, one has $Gg = G$ ($Gg = \{g_i g \mid g_i \in G\}$). Indeed, every $g_1 \in G$ is obtainable as a product $g_1 g^{-1} \cdot g = g_1$, and $g_1 g^{-1}$ is equal to some g_i.

If G is a group and H a subgroup of G, then Ha, where $a \in G$, is called a *right coset* of H in G. Assume $c \in Ha \cap Hb$. Then there exists an $h \in H$ such that $c = ha$, i.e.,

$$a = h^{-1}c \quad \text{and} \quad Ha = Hh^{-1}c = Hc.$$

In the same way $Hb = Hc$, i.e., if two right cosets of H in G have a common element, they coincide, otherwise they are disjoint. All elements in a right coset of H in G are distinct

$$h_1 a = h_2 a \Rightarrow h_1 = h_2.$$

Hence, every right coset of H has $|H|$ elements. Finally, every element $g \in G$ belongs to some right coset: $g \in Hg$, because $g = eg$.

It follows from the above that the right cosets of H are blocks of a partition of G. Every such block has the same number of elements $|H|$, and every element of a block defines the entire block, because, as was shown,

$$c \in Ha \Rightarrow Ha = Hc.$$

Every block has $|H|$ elements, hence $|G|/|H|$ is the number of blocks. This number is also called the index of H in G. A very important result of the above discussion is the following theorem :

THEOREM.   In a finite group G the order of every subgroup H divides the order of the group.

It follows that a group of prime order cannot have nontrivial subgroups. Every noncyclic group has such subgroups; hence, there are only cyclic groups of prime orders, i.e., for every prime p there is, up to isomorphism, exactly one group of order p—the cyclic one.

1.14   Normal Subgroups. Simple Groups

The equivalence R over a group G corresponding to the partition into right cosets of a subgroup H is a right congruence, because $a\ R\ b \Rightarrow \exists\ x$ such that

$$a, b \in Hx \Rightarrow ag, bg \in (Hx)g = H(xg) \Rightarrow ag\ R\ bg \qquad \text{for any}\quad g \in H.$$

R is, in general, not a congruence, i.e., the partition of a group G into right cosets of a subgroup H is, in general, not admissible. A corresponding example was presented in Section 1.10: the partition of S_3 into right cosets of the subgroup $H = \{e, b\}$ is not admissible.

On the other hand, such a partition will always be admissible if G is a commutative group. Indeed, in this case,

$$Ha \cdot Hb = HHab = Hab$$

i.e., the product of two right cosets (in this case there is no need to distinguish right from left) is again a right coset of H in G.

The same situation may also occur with some subgroups in non-commutative groups. In S_3 mentioned above, the right cosets of the subgroup $H = \{e, a, a^2\}$ are

$$H = \{e, a, a^2\} \qquad \text{and} \qquad Hb = \{b, c. d\},$$

and they form an admissible partition of S_3. A subgroup H of G is called a *normal subgroup* if its right cosets constitute an admissible partition of G.

Every trivial subgroup is normal, every commutative group has only normal subgroups; there are also noncommutative groups which have nontrivial normal subgroups.

A group which has only trivial normal subgroups is called a *simple group*. A commutative group is thus simple if and only if it is a cyclic group of prime order. But there are also noncommutative simple groups. It is proved that such a group must be of even order. The smallest simple noncommutative group is of order 60; this is the group of all even permutations of five objects. In general, a group of all even permutations of five or more objects is simple. Other noncommutative simple groups are also known, but investigation of this topic is far from being finished. Simple groups will be extensively mentioned in Chapter 7.

If H is normal in G, its right cosets coincide with the left ones, i.e., $Ha = aH$. Indeed, if the partition into right cosets is admissible, then $a^{-1}Ha$ must be a right coset of H ($a^{-1}Ha$ must be included in a right coset, but $|a^{-1}Ha| = |H|$; hence, it is a complete right coset). But $e \in a^{-1}Ha$, so that this right coset is H itself. From $a^{-1}Ha = H$ follows $Ha = aH$. And, vice versa, if for every a in G, $a^{-1}Ha = H$, i.e., $Ha = aH$, then H is normal in G because $HaHb = HHab = Hab$, i.e., the product of two right cosets is a right coset.

Given a group G and a normal subgroup H, one can use the admissible partition π of G into (right) cosets of H to build the factor group G/π. This group is usually denoted G/H and its elements are the blocks of π, i.e., the cosets of H in G. The natural homomorphism φ of G onto G/H maps H onto the identity of G/H.

Now let φ be a homomorphism of G onto a group G_1. The set of elements of G mapped by φ onto the identity e_1 of G_1 forms a subgroup H of G. Indeed,

$$a\varphi = e_1, \, b\varphi = e_1 \Rightarrow (ab)\varphi = a\varphi b\varphi = e_1 e_1 = e_1$$

and

$$a^{-1}\varphi = (a\varphi)^{-1} = e_1^{-1} = e_1.$$

Moreover, H is a normal subgroup of G. To show this, notice that

$$(a^{-1}Ha)\varphi = a^{-1}\varphi \cdot H\varphi \cdot a\varphi = (a\varphi)^{-1}e_1 a\varphi = e_1,$$

i.e., $a^{-1}Ha \subseteq H$ for any a. This implies $Ha \subseteq aH$, and, as both have $|H|$ elements, $Ha = aH$ as required.

To summarize:

THEOREM.   To every normal subgroup H of G there corresponds a factor group G/H which is a homomorphic image of G, and, conversely, given a homomorphism φ of G onto G_1, the set of elements mapped by φ onto the identity of G_1 forms a normal subgroup H of G (the so-called *kernel* of φ).

Exactly as in Section 1.11, one shows also that G_1 is isomorphic to G/H.

It follows that a simple group has only two (up to isomorphism, of course) homomorphic images: itself, this is actually an isomorphism, and the one-element group. Every other group has nontrivial homomorphic images.

Finally, notice that $|G/H| = |G|/|H|$.

1.15   Direct Product of Groups. Homomorphisms onto Simple Groups

The following facts will be used in Chapter 7.

LEMMA A.   Let K be a group and φ a homomorphism of K onto a simple group H. If K_1 is a normal subgroup of K, then $K_1\varphi = e_H$ (the identity of H) or $K_1\varphi = H$.

Proof. Let $K_1\varphi = H_1$. H_1 is a homomorphic image of a group; hence, H_1 is a group—a subgroup of H. For every $h \in H$ take a $k \in h\varphi^{-1}$ (k is one of the elements of K mapped by φ onto h), and notice that $k^{-1}K_1k = K_1$ (because K_1 is a normal subgroup of K). Hence, $k^{-1}\varphi K_1\varphi k\varphi = K_1\varphi$, i.e., $h^{-1}H_1h = H_1$. This is true for every $h \in H$, consequently, H_1 is normal in H. But H is simple; hence, H_1 is e_H or H.

LEMMA B.   With the same assumptions as in Lemma A, H is a homomorphic image of K_1 or of K/K_1.

Proof. If $K_1\varphi = H$, there is nothing to prove. Assume $K_1\varphi = e_H$. It follows that K_1 is a subgroup of the kernel K_2 of φ. Since K_1 is normal in K it is normal in any subgroup of K containing it; hence, also in K_2. (K_1 normal in K implies $k^{-1}K_1k = K_1$ for all $k \in K$, in particular, for all $k \in K_2 \Rightarrow K_1$ is normal in K_2.) Now, the situation is exactly as in Section 1.11, where the induced homomorphism was presented, and K/K_2 is a homomorphic image of K/K_1. But $H \simeq K/K_2$; hence, H is a homomorphic image of K/K_1.

The direct product $F \times G$ of two groups F and G is the set of all pairs $(f; g), f \in F, g \in G$, with the operation defined as follows:

$$(f_1; g_1)(f_2; g_2) = (f_1f_2; g_1g_2).$$

$F \times G$ is, clearly, a semigroup; moreover, (e_F, e_G) serves as an identity and $(f^{-1}; g^{-1})$ is the inverse of $(f; g)$. Hence, $F \times G$ is a group. The set of elements of $F \times G$ of the form $(f; e_G)$, $f \in F$, forms a subgroup $(F; e_G)$ of $F \times G$ isomorphic to F. This subgroup is normal in $F \times G$, because

$$(f; g)^{-1}(F; e_G)(f; g) = (f^{-1}Ff; g^{-1}e_Gg) = (F; e_G).$$

By symmetry the set of pairs $(e_F; G)$ is a normal subgroup of $F \times G$ isomorphic to G.

One can, in an obvious way, define a direct product of three, four, or any finite number of groups.

LEMMA C.   Let F and G be groups and K a subgroup of their direct product $F \times G$. Then K is an extension of a group isomorphic to a subgroup A of F by a group isomorphic to a subgroup B of G.

Proof. K is called an *extension* of A_k by B_k if A_k is a normal subgroup of K and $B_k \simeq K/A_k$.

Let $A_k = \{(f, e_G)\}$, where $f \in F$ and $(f, e_G) \in K$; A_k is a subgroup of K, even a normal one. A_k is also isomorphic to a subgroup A of F. Now,

$$(f_1, g_1) \in A_k(f_2, g_2) \Leftrightarrow g_1 g_2^{-1} = e_G, \qquad \text{that is} \quad g_1 = g_2.$$

Hence, every right coset of A_k in K is characterized by the unique second component (second element in the pair) of its elements. $B_k = K/A_k$ is thus isomorphic to a subgroup B of G consisting of those components (which are elements of G, of course).

LEMMA D.   Let K be a subgroup of the direct product $F \times G$ of two groups and let φ be a homomorphism of K onto a simple group H. Then H is a homomorphic image of a subgroup of F or of a subgroup of G.

Proof. K is an extension of a group A_k isomorphic to a subgroup A of F by a group B_k isomorphic to a subgroup B of G. Hence, A_k is normal in K and $B_k \simeq K/A_k$. By Lemma B, the simple group H being a homomorphic image of K must be a homomorphic image of A_k or of B_k, i.e., also of A or of B.

1.16   Some Properties of Semigroups

Some additional notions and facts from the theory of semigroups will be of great help later.

Let P be a *finite* semigroup and $p \in P$. Among the powers $p, p^2, p^3, \ldots$

there must be two equal (P is finite). Let p^j be the smallest power of p equal to a previous power of p, say p^i.

Denote $j - i = m$. Now, from $p^i = p^j$ one obtains

$$p^i = p^{i+m} = p^i p^m = p^{i+m} p^m = \cdots = p^{i+sm}$$

for any nonnegative integer s. For any $k \geq j$ one has $k = i + tm + r$, where $r < m$; hence,

$$p^k = p^{i+tm+r} = p^{i+r}.$$

In words, every p^k with $k \geq j$ (actually with $k \geq i$) is equal to p^{i+r} where $0 \leq r < m$. It follows that the elements

$$p, p^2, \ldots, p^{i-1}, p^i, p^{i+1}, \ldots, p^{i+m-1}$$

form a subsemigroup of P called the *cyclic* semigroup generated by p in P. The m consecutive powers $p^i, p^{i+1}, \ldots, p^{i+m-1}$ form a cyclic group Z of order m. To prove this, notice first that Z is closed under multiplication (as proved, p^k for any $k \geq i$ is equal to some element from Z). Next, one of the m consecutive integers $i, i + 1, \ldots, i + m - 1$ is a multiple of m, say $i + t = xm$ ($t < m$). Then

$$p^{i+r} p^{i+t} = p^{i+r} p^{xm} = p^{i+xm+r} = p^{i+r},$$

i.e., p^{i+t} is an identity in Z. Finally, for any r, take a y big enough so that $ym - i - r > i$ and $y > x$. Then p^{ym-i-r} is equal to some element of Z and

$$p^{i+r} p^{ym-i-r} = p^{i+(y-x)m+xm+r-i-r} = p^{i+xm+r-i-r} = p^{xm},$$

i.e., p^{ym-i-r} is the inverse of p^{i+r}. Thus, Z is a group. Notice $p^{xm+r} p^{xm+1} = p^{xm+r+1}$, which shows that Z can be generated by the element p^{xm+1}, i.e., Z is cyclic.

An important corollary is that in a finite semigroup every element must have a power which is idempotent (the identity of the above Z).

There follow three theorems dealing with semigroups.

THEOREM A.   For every homomorphism φ of a finite semigroup P onto a group G, there exists a subgroup (i.e., a subsemigroup which is a group) K of P such that $K\varphi = G$.

Proof.   Let E be the set of idempotents of P. Choose $e \in E$ such that Pe has the smallest possible number of elements. (Notice that unlike for a group, for a semigroup P one may have Pp $(p \in P)$ included *properly* in P.) $K = ePe$ is a subsemigroup of P, because

$$ep_1e \cdot ep_2e = e(p_1ep_2)e = ep_3e \qquad (p_1, p_2, p_3 \in P).$$

Now,

$$e \cdot epe = epe, \; epe \cdot e = epe,$$
i.e., e is an identity in K.
   Let $f \in K \cap E$. Then $f = ep_1e$ $(p_1 \in P)$ and

$$Pf = Pep_1e \subseteq Pe \Rightarrow Pf = Pe$$

(Pe has the smallest possible number of elements for all idempotents in E),

$$e = ee \in Pe = Pf \Rightarrow e = p_2f \qquad (p_2 \in P).$$

Hence,

$$e = p_2f = p_2ff = ef = eep_1e = ep_1e = f,$$

that is, e is the unique idempotent in K.
   Now, for every $epe \in K$ there exists an n such that $(epe)^n$ is an idempotent, that is, e. Hence,

$$(epe)(epe)^{n-1} = (epe)^{n-1}(epe) = e,$$

and $(epe)^{n-1}$ serves as an inverse of epe with respect to e; K is, consequently, a group.
   The remaining assertion follows immediately, because

$$K\varphi = (ePe)\varphi = e\varphi P\varphi e\varphi = e_G G e_G = G.$$

(Every idempotent of P must be mapped onto the unique idempotent in G: e_G.)

THEOREM B. Let G be a semigroup of mappings of a finite set S and let K be a subgroup of G. Then there exists a subset S_0 of S such that the restrictions of the elements of K to S_0 are permutations forming a group isomorphic to K.

Proof. A restriction of a mapping φ to a subset S_0 of $pr_1\varphi$ is the mapping $I_{S_0}\varphi$, i.e., this "part" of φ which is applied to elements of S_0 only. Now the proof.

Set $S_0 = Se_K = pr_2e_K$.

$$e_Ke_K = e_K \Rightarrow \left(\binom{a}{b} \in e_K \Rightarrow \binom{b}{b} \in e_K\right),$$

thus e_K restricted to S_0 is the identity on S_0.

If $a \in S_0$ and $\binom{a}{b} \in x \in K$, then $xx^{-1} = e_K$, and since e_K must include

$\binom{a}{a}$, $\binom{b}{a} \in x^{-1}$. But then $e_K = x^{-1}x$ includes $\binom{b}{b}$, and thus $b \in S_0$.

Hence, $x \in K \Rightarrow S_0x \subseteq S_0$. But $a, b \in S_0$, $x \in K$, and $\binom{ab}{cc} \in x \Rightarrow \nexists\, y \in K$

such that $xy = e_K$. This proves that $S_0x = S_0$, i.e., the restriction x_0 of x to S_0 is a permutation of the elements of S_0. $x = y \Rightarrow x_0 = y_0$, but also, $x_0 = y_0 \Rightarrow x = y$, because

$$x = e_Kx = e_Kx_0 = e_Ky_0 = e_Ky = y$$

(notice, $e_Kx = e_Kx_0$, because $pr_2e_K = S_0$).

Finally, $xy = z \Rightarrow x_0y_0 \subseteq z$, but x_0y_0 is a permutation of S_0, hence $x_0y_0 = z_0$.

Thus, the theorem is proved.

THEOREM C. Let G be a semigroup of mappings of a finite set S, and assume that there exists a subset S_0 of S such that some elements of G

when restricted to S_0 are permutations. Then there exists in G a subgroup G_2 such that the permutation group G_0, generated by the above-mentioned permutations of S_0, is a homomorphic image of G_2.

Proof.   Denote by T the subset of G composed of all mappings such that their restriction to S_0 is a permutation. T is closed under multiplication; hence, T is a subsemigroup of G. Denote by e an idempotent in T with a minimal possible number of elements in Te over the necessarily nonempty set of idempotents in T. Denote by G_1 the subsemigroup eTe of T. Exactly as in proof of Theorem A one obtains that G_1 is a group—a subgroup of T, hence, also of G. Notice also that all permutations of S_0 appearing in the mappings of T will appear in the mappings of G_1, too.

Denote by G_2 the subgroup of G_1 generated by those elements of G_1 which, when restricted to S_0, are permutations appearing in G_0. G_2 is a subgroup of G_1, hence, also of G; the mapping φ of G_2 into G_0, such that for every $g_2 \in G_2$, $g_2\varphi$ is the element of G_0 performing the same permutation of S_0 as g_2 does, is, clearly, a homomorphism of G_2 onto G_0. This concludes the proof of the theorem.

1.17   Universal Algebras

Groupoids are examples of binary multiplicative systems—sets with one binary operation. One often encounters systems with more than one operation and systems with operations which are not binary. The following notion of a *universal algebra* provides a convenient framework to deal with such systems.

Let A be a set. One says that an n-ary (n being a nonnegative integer) algebraic operation w is defined in A if there is given a law assigning to every n-tuple $(a_1, a_2, \ldots, a_n)$ of elements of A a unique element of A which will be denoted by $a_1 a_2 \ldots a_n w$.

A set A with a system of n-ary algebraic operations (n may be different from operation to operation) is called a *universal algebra*.

The operations can be *binary*, *ternary*, etc., but also *unary*, which means a mapping of A into A. A *nullary* operation means choosing a constant element of A.

For example, a group can be considered as a universal algebra with an associative binary operation of multiplication, a unary operation of taking an inverse, and a nullary operation of choosing the identity.

A groupoid is a universal algebra with one binary operation.

A subalgebra A_1 of A is defined as a subset $A_1 \subseteq A$ such that for every n-ary operation w in A:

$$a_1, a_2, \ldots, a_n \in A_1 \Rightarrow a_1 a_2 \ldots a_n w \in A_1$$

(i.e., A_1 is closed under the operations in A). The notions of homomorphism and isomorphism can be defined in an obvious way for pairs of general algebras which have operations of the same kind (i.e., when there exists a one-to-one correspondence between the operations in both algebras such that to every n-ary operation in one there corresponds an n-ary operation in the other, with the same n).

In the same manner, one can define congruence relations over A, or what is the same admissible partitions of A. The factor algebra A/π (π an admissible partition) can be defined similarly, and the homomorphism theorem holds also in this general case.

The intersection of admissible partitions is an admissible partition. If $\pi_1 \leq \pi_2$, then A/π_2 is a homomorphic image of A/π_1.

The reader will provide the proofs of the above facts without difficulty, some of them will be used in the next chapter.

Chapter 2

Semiautomata

2.1 Definition and Representation of a Semiautomaton

Many physical devices have the remarkable property of tending to remain in any of a finite number of situations or *states*. The "jumping" from one state to another (sometimes the same) is a continuous process which must be very carefully considered by the designer of the device, but can be disregarded by the user interested only in the above discrete states.

Examples range from an electronic computer and chess play, through the inventory list of a factory and the distribution of manpower of a company, to traffic light and the ringing of a bell.

In order to single out the above feature common to so many and distinct devices, the following mathematical notion was introduced:

DEFINITION.   A (deterministic) *semiautomaton* (also called completely specified deterministic semiautomaton) is a triple $A = (S, \Sigma, M)$, where

$$S = \{s_0, s_1, \ldots, s_{n-1}\}$$

is a finite set (of *states* of A),

$$\Sigma = \{\sigma_0, \sigma_1, \ldots, \sigma_{m-1}\}$$

is a finite set (of *inputs* of A), and

$$M = \{M_{\sigma_0}, M_{\sigma_1}, \ldots, M_{\sigma_{m-1}}\}$$

is a set of mappings of S into S (every M_{σ_i} is such a mapping).
For example,

$$A = \left(\{1, 2, 3, 4, 5, 6\}, \{\sigma_0, \sigma_1\},\right.$$

$$\left.\left\{M_{\sigma_0} = \begin{pmatrix} 1 & 2 & 3 & 4 & 5 & 6 \\ 3 & 1 & 2 & 1 & 3 & 5 \end{pmatrix}, \quad M_{\sigma_1} = \begin{pmatrix} 1 & 2 & 3 & 4 & 5 & 6 \\ 4 & 5 & 3 & 3 & 3 & 3 \end{pmatrix}\right\}\right)$$

is a semiautomaton with six states and two inputs.

A semiautomaton is often described by means of a table (also called next state table or transition table), which, for the previous example, will have the following form:

The states of A

	1	2	3	4	5	6
A						
σ_0	3	1	2	1	3	5
σ_1	4	5	3	3	3	3

The inputs of A

Still another representation of semiautomata is extremely useful. It uses a directed graph. The vertices of the graph represent the states of A, and for every $\begin{pmatrix} s_i \\ s_j \end{pmatrix} \in M_{\sigma_k}$ an arrow labeled σ_k leads from s_i to s_j. For the above A one obtains

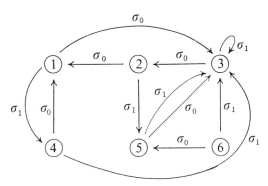

All descriptions of A fulfill their aim very transparently: they list the states and inputs of A and indicate clearly the state to which A will go if it is in state s_i and receives an input σ_j. Each representation has its advantages and will be used appropriately.

The notion of semiautomaton, so simply defined and easily described, serves as a basis for a rich and interesting theory, some parts of which will be discussed in the sequel.

Notice that a semiautomaton can be considered as a universal algebra over the finite set S with a unary operation corresponding to every element of Σ. Thus, algebraic notions and methods will be very useful in dealing with semiautomata.

2.2   The Semigroup of a Semiautomaton

Consider, as in Sections 1.3 and 1.12, the free semigroup Σ^*. To every word $x = \sigma_{i_1}\sigma_{i_2}\ldots\sigma_{i_k}$ of Σ^* there corresponds the mapping $M_x = M_{\sigma_{i_1}}M_{\sigma_{i_2}}\ldots M_{\sigma_{i_k}}$ of S into S: if A is in state s_i and the sequence of inputs constituting x is applied to the semiautomaton, it will go to the state $M_x(s_i) = s_i M_x$. $M_\wedge$ is the identity over S. The relation E over Σ^* defined by:

$$x \, E \, y \Leftrightarrow M_x = M_y$$

is a congruence (cf. 1.12): its congruence classes are composed of all words in Σ^* inducing equal mappings of S into S. The index of E is finite because S is finite, and there is only a finite number of distinct mappings of S into S.

G_A, the finite monoid of mappings generated by the mappings in M and by $M_\wedge$ is called *the semigroup of the semiautomaton*. Clearly, $G_A \simeq \Sigma^*/E$.

On the other hand, given a finite monoid G, one can construct a semiautomaton A having G as its semigroup. To this end let the elements of G be the states of A and Σ will be a set of generators of G (one can take the entire G). M_σ will be the right translation of G corresponding to σ, i.e., for every $g \in G$, $gM_\sigma = g\sigma$. The semigroup G_A of

A, i.e., the semigroup generated by the mappings M_σ will be isomorphic to G, as shown in Section 1.5.

The A constructed above is not the only semiautomaton having G as its semigroup. As will be seen, there is no difficulty in finding examples of distinct semiautomata having isomorphic semigroups.

2.3   Right Congruences over Σ^* and the Corresponding Semiautomata

It was shown in Section 2.2. that a semiautomaton A induces a congruence relation with a finite index over the free semigroup Σ^*. On the other hand, a *right* congruence over Σ^* is enough to enable a definition of a related semiautomaton. Indeed, assume that a right congruence relation E_r with a finite index is given over Σ^*. It determines a "corresponding" semiautomaton A in the following way: the states of A are the congruence classes of E_r (there is a finite number of such classes); the inputs of A are the generators of Σ^*, i.e., the elements of Σ; the mapping M_{σ_i} is defined using representatives, i.e., if s_j is the congruence class containing $x \in \Sigma^*$, then $s_j M_{\sigma_i}$ will be the class containing $x\sigma_i \in \Sigma^*$. This is a proper definition because $x \, E_r \, y \Rightarrow x\sigma_i \, E_r \, y\sigma_i$ (E_r is a right congruence).

The semiautomaton A has the following special property:

Let s_0 denote the congruence class of E_r containing $\wedge$. If s_i contains $x \in \Sigma^*$, then $s_0 M_x = s_i$ because $\wedge x = x$. It follows that to every state of A there corresponds at least one input word taking s_0 into this state. Such a semiautomaton is called a *cyclic semiautomaton* and s_0 is called its generator.

The graph of a cyclic semiautomaton contains at least one vertex such that every vertex can be reached from it by a directed path, i.e., a path following the arrows.

2.4   Subsemiautomata.   Homomorphism

In what follows σ_i^A will be often used to denote the mapping M_{σ_i} in the semiautomaton A.

DEFINITION.   A semiautomaton $B = (S^B, \Sigma^B, M^B)$ is said to be a
subsemiautomaton of the semiautomaton $A = (S^A, \Sigma^A, M^A)$ if $S^B \subseteq S^A$,
$\Sigma^B \subseteq \Sigma^A$, and $\sigma_i^B \subseteq \sigma_i^A$ for every $\sigma_i \in \Sigma^B$.

Notice that unlike the definition of a subalgebra of a universal
algebra, here some of the operations in A may be omitted in the subsemiautomaton B.

It follows that every subset S^B of S^A closed under a subset M^B of
mappings of M^A forms a subsemiautomaton of A. A typical example for
such a situation is the case when the graph of A is not connected; i.e., it
is composed of several parts (components) such that there is no seg-
ment leading from one to the other. Every component of the graph
describes a subsemiautomaton of A, with $\Sigma^B = \Sigma^A$. Those states of a
semiautomaton A which can be reached from a particular state s_i form,
also, a subsemiautomaton of A—a cyclic one—with $\Sigma^B = \Sigma^A$, and s_i as
generator.

Every A with $|\Sigma^A| \geq 2$ has proper subsemiautomata—take $S^B = S^A$
and Σ^B a proper subset of Σ^A. On the other hand, for $|\Sigma^A| = 1$, say
$\Sigma^A = \{\sigma_0\}$, there exist semiautomata without proper subsemiautomata.
The reader should convince himself that this is the case if and only if the
corresponding σ_0^A is a cycle as in the figure:

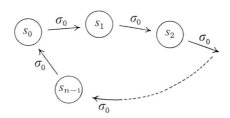

LEMMA.   The semigroup G_B of the subsemiautomaton B of A is a
homomorphic image of a subsemigroup of G_A.

Proof.   The mappings σ_i^A such that $\sigma_i \in \Sigma^B$ and the identity generator
a subsemigroup G of G_A (because these mappings form a subset of the
generators of G_A). The restrictions of the elements of G to S^B are

mappings of S^B into S^B, and they form the semigroup G_B. Now, the mapping φ of G onto G_B defined by

$$g\varphi = \text{the restriction of} \quad g \quad \text{to } S^B \qquad (g \in G)$$

is a homomorphism because $(g_1 g_2)\varphi = (g_1\varphi)(g_2\varphi)$. Notice that φ need not be one-to-one: $g_1 \neq g_2$ may coincide on S^B and then $g_1\varphi = g_2\varphi$. In the case when $\Sigma^B = \Sigma^A$, G_B is a homomorphic image of G_A.

DEFINITION.   The semiautomaton $B = (S^B, \Sigma^B, M^B)$ is a homomorphic image of the semiautomaton $A = (S^A, \Sigma^A, M^A)$ if there exist a mapping φ of S^A onto S^B and a mapping ξ of Σ^A onto Σ^B such that for every $\sigma \in \Sigma^A$, $\sigma^A \varphi = \varphi(\sigma\xi)^B$.

Notice the complete analogy to the definition of homomorphism in groupoids: the operation and mapping must commute $[(ab)_\varphi = (a\varphi)(b\varphi)]$.

In most applications ξ will be one-to-one; then Σ^B can be renamed, if necessary, to be equal to Σ^A, and ξ is the identity. In this case one requires

$$\sigma^A\varphi = \varphi\sigma^B \qquad \text{for all } \cdot\sigma \in \Sigma^A.$$

If φ is also one-to-one the semiautomata A and B are *isomorphic* and can be obtained one from the other by merely renaming the states and the inputs.

The equivalence relation $\varphi\varphi^{-1}$ divides S^A into equivalence classes—blocks of the corresponding partition π, so that $s, t \in S^A$ are in the same block if and only if $s\varphi = t\varphi$. But then for every $\sigma \in \Sigma^A$

$$s\sigma^A\varphi = s\varphi(\sigma\xi)^B = t\varphi(\sigma\xi)^B = t\sigma^A\varphi$$

i.e., $s\sigma^A$ and $t\sigma^A$ also belong to one block of π. Thus, every homomorphism φ of A induces an admissible partition π of S^A.

Conversely, let $\pi = \{H_0, H_1, \ldots, H_{p-1}\}$ be a partition of S^A. The partition is admissible if for every $\sigma \in \Sigma^A$ and every $H_i \in \pi$ there exists an $H_j \in \pi$ such that $H_i\sigma^A \subseteq H_j$. Then the semiautomaton B, in which the states are the blocks of π (in this role they will be denoted by $\bar{H}_i$), which has the same inputs as A, and in which for every $\sigma \in \Sigma^B = \Sigma^A$

$$\bar{H}_i \sigma^B = \bar{H}_j \Leftrightarrow H_i \sigma^A \subseteq H_j,$$

is a homomorphic image of A with $s\varphi = \bar{H}_i \Leftrightarrow s \in H_i$, and ξ being the identity. One denotes $B = A/\pi$ and calls B the quotient semiautomaton of A over π.

Two admissible partitions exist in every A:

1. The identity partition π_{iden} in which every state of S forms a block itself—the corresponding semiautomaton B is isomorphic to A.
2. The partition π_0 in which all elements of S form one block. B is in this case a one-state semiautomaton.

There are semiautomata which have only these two trivial admissible partitions. Altogether, everything said in Chapter 1 about partitions and, in particular, about admissible partitions, holds for the case of semiautomata.

2.5   Homomorphisms of One-Input Semiautomata

Determination of all homomorphic images of a semiautomaton A is equivalent to constructing all admissible partitions of its state set S. For the case when $|\Sigma| = 1$ ($\Sigma = \{\sigma\}$), this can be done in the following way [47].

Notice, first, that every component of the graph of such a semiautomaton must contain a single cycle. G_A is a cyclic semigroup and its elements are powers of $\sigma^A = \sigma$ (A will be omitted for simplicity). The states of a cycle of length k in the graph can thus be described in the form:

$$s = s\sigma^0, s\sigma, s\sigma^2, \ldots, s\sigma^{k-1}.$$

s is one (an arbitrary) state in the cycle.

Now, the following types of partitions of S will be called elementary:

Type π_α.   Let S have a cycle as above and let p be a prime divisor of k. Then $s\sigma^i \, \pi_\alpha \, s\sigma^j \Leftrightarrow i \equiv j(\mathrm{mod}\ k/p)$. Every state outside the considered cycle forms a block of π_α by itself.

Type π_β.   Let s and t be states such that $s\sigma = t\sigma$. Then $s \, \pi_\beta \, t$ (and all other states of S form blocks consisting of singletons).

Type π_γ.   Let C_1 and C_2 be different cycles, both of length k, and let s_1, s_2 be arbitrary vertices of C_1, C_2, respectively. Then $s_1\sigma^j \, \pi_\gamma \, s_2\sigma^j$, $j = 0, 1, \ldots, k - 1$ (and, as in the previous cases, all states beside C_1 and C_2 each form a distinct block of π_γ).

Any partition of one of the above types is, clearly, admissible. The following theorem justifies the name: elementary partition.

THEOREM.   An admissible partition $\pi \neq \pi_{\mathrm{iden}}$ of S in a one-input semiautomaton is elementary if and only if for every admissible partition $\pi' \neq \pi$ of S:

$$\pi' \leq \pi \Rightarrow \pi' = \pi_{\mathrm{iden}}.$$

Proof.   If π is an elementary partition it cannot include properly any admissible partition distinct from the identity. This is quite evident for π_β, but, also, for π_α and π_γ one easily checks that the inclusion of any two elements appearing in one block of π_α or of π_γ into a common block implies (because of the admissibility requirement) the complete structure of these partitions.

Conversely, assume $\pi \neq \pi_{\mathrm{iden}}$ and there is no $\pi' \neq \pi_{\mathrm{iden}}$ such that π' is properly finer than π. There exist two states s, $t \in S$ such that $s \, \pi \, t$. Now consider the following cases:

Case A.   There exists a positive integer h such that $s\sigma^h = t\sigma^h$. Then the admissible partition π' defined by: $s\sigma^{h-1} \, \pi' \, t\sigma^{h-1}$ is elementary of type π_β and $\pi \geq \pi' \neq \pi_{\mathrm{iden}}$. Hence, $\pi = \pi'$.

Case B.   There exists a nonnegative integer h such that $s\sigma^h = u \neq$

$v = t\sigma^h$, and u, v are both on the same cycle C (of length k). Let $v = u\sigma^m$, and let d be the greatest common divisor of m and k. The states

$$u, u\sigma^d, u\sigma^{2d}, \ldots, u\sigma^{(m/d)\cdot d} = v, \ldots, u\sigma^{(k/d-1)d}$$

of C belong to a block H of π.

Let p be a prime number dividing k/d. Define an admissible partition π' of type π_a by:

$$u\sigma^i \ \pi' \ u\sigma^j \Leftrightarrow i \equiv j \,(\text{mod } k/p).$$

The states $u, u\sigma^{k/p}, u\sigma^{2k/p}, \ldots, u\sigma^{(p-1)k/p}$ form a block K of π'. Since $k/d = pa$ for some integer a, $k/p = ad$ and $K \subseteq H$.

Similarly, any other block of π' is included in a block of π hence $\pi' \leq \pi$. But $\pi' \neq \pi_{\text{iden}}$, so that $\pi = \pi'$ and thus π is elementary.

Case C. The states s and t belong to two different components of the graph of A, containing cycles C_1 and C_2 of length k_1 and k_2, respectively. Then there exists a nonnegative integer h such that $s\sigma^h = u \ \pi \ v = t\sigma^h$ and $u \in C_1$, $v \in C_2$. Let d be the greatest common divisor of k_1 and k_2. If, say, $k_1 > d$, then the nontrivial admissible partition π' given by

$$u\sigma^i \ \pi' \ u\sigma^j \Leftrightarrow i \equiv j (\text{mod } d)$$

is properly included in π. Hence, $k_1 = k_2 = d$, and the elementary partition π'' of type π_γ merging cycles C_1 and C_2 satisfies $\pi \geq \pi'' \neq \pi_{\text{iden}}$. Therefore, $\pi = \pi''$, i.e., π is elementary.

The theorem is proved. From it follows, by construction of induced homomorphisms (cf. 1.11), the theorem:

THEOREM.   If A' is a homomorphic image of a one-input semiautomaton A, there exists a series

$$A = A_0, A_1, \ldots, A_r \simeq A'$$

such that A_{i+1} ($i = 0, 1, \ldots, r-1$) is a homomorphic image of A_i and the corresponding admissible partition is elementary.

This provides a direct method of deriving all admissible partitions, hence, all homomorphic images of a one-input semiautomaton. It would be desirable to have a solution of this kind for the multiple-input semiautomata. Of course, the problem is solvable, since in the finite case all possible partitions can be examined. There exist techniques which allow the work to be considerably shortened, but still more efficient methods will be extremely useful.

2.6 Semiautomata and the Corresponding Congruences over Σ^*

Let E be the congruence over Σ^* induced by the semiautomaton A. The semigroup G_A of A is isomorphic to Σ^*/E.

The construction in Section 2.3 applied to the congruence E leads to a corresponding semiautomaton A'. Then A and A' have the same set of inputs Σ, but, in general, they are not isomorphic. Indeed, A' is cyclic no matter what A will be.

THEOREM. Let A_1 be any cyclic subsemiautomaton of A with the generator s_1 and the same set of inputs; then A_1 is a homomorphic image of A'.

Proof. Define a mapping φ as follows: if s' is a state of A' corresponding to the congruence class of E containing the word x, put $s'\varphi = s_1 x^{A_1}$ ($x^{A_1} = M_x$ in A_1). For every $y \in \Sigma^*$ in the same congruence class

$$s_1 y^{A_1} = s_1 y^A = s_1 x^A = s_1 x^{A_1}.$$

(A_1 is a subsemiautomaton of A; hence, $s_1 x^A = s_1 x^{A_1}$. Additionally, $\begin{pmatrix} x \\ y \end{pmatrix} \in E \Rightarrow s_1 x^A = s_1 y^A$.) Therefore, φ is well-defined. It is a mapping onto the states of A_1 because A_1 is cyclic with the generator s_1. Finally, with ξ equal to the identity, one gets for every $\sigma \in \Sigma$ and every state s' of A': if the class of s' contains x, then

$$s'\varphi\sigma^{A_1} = s_1 x^{A_1}\sigma^{A_1} = s_1(x\sigma)^{A_1} = s''\varphi,$$

where the class of s'' contains $x\sigma$, i.e., $s'' = s'\sigma^{A'}$. Thus, for every state s' of A':

$$s'\varphi\sigma^{A_1} = s'\sigma^{A'}\varphi, \qquad \text{that is} \qquad \varphi\sigma^{A_1} = \sigma^{A'}\varphi$$

and A_1 is a homomorphic image of A'. Obviously, if A itself is cyclic, then A is a homomorphic image of A'.

Let $A = (S, \Sigma, M)$ be any semiautomaton and $s \in S$. Define the following relation $E(s)$ over Σ^*:

$$x\, E(s)\, y \Leftrightarrow sx^A = sy^A.$$

$E(s)$ is a right congruence relation: $E(s)$ is clearly an equivalence and for every $z \in \Sigma^*$:

$$x\, E(s)\, y \Rightarrow sx^A = sy^A \Rightarrow$$

$$sx^A z^A = sy^A z^A \Rightarrow$$

$$s(xz)^A = s(yz)^A \Rightarrow xz\, E(s)\, yz.$$

The semiautomaton A' corresponding to $E(s)$ by the construction in Section 2.3 is *isomorphic* to the cyclic subsemiautomaton A_1 of A generated by s. Indeed, by the same proof as above, A_1 is a homomorphic image of A', but this time: $s' \neq t'$ in A', i.e., $x\, E\,(s)\, y$, where x and y are words in the equivalence classes s' and t', respectively, implies $sx^A \neq sy^A$, i.e., $s'\varphi \neq t'\varphi$ and, consequently, φ is one-to-one.

2.7   The Homomorphism of Semigroups of Homomorphic Semiautomata

THEOREM.   If B is a homomorphic image of A, then the semigroup G_B of B is a homomorphic image of the semigroup G_A of A.

Proof. Let $B = (S^B, \Sigma^B, M^B)$ be a homomorphic image of $A = (S^A, \Sigma^A, M^A)$; i.e., φ and ξ exist such that for every $\sigma \in \Sigma^A$:

$$\sigma^A \varphi = \varphi(\sigma\xi)^B.$$

It follows:

$$x^A\varphi = \sigma_{i_1}^A\sigma_{i_2}^A\ldots\sigma_{i_k}^A\varphi = \sigma_{i_1}^A\sigma_{i_2}^A\ldots\sigma_{i_{k-1}}^A\varphi(\sigma_{i_k}\xi)^B$$
$$= \varphi(\sigma_{i_1}\xi)^B(\sigma_{i_2}\xi)^B\ldots(\sigma_{i_k}\xi)^B = \varphi(x\xi)^B,$$

where $x\xi = (\sigma_{i_1}\xi)(\sigma_{i_2}\xi)\ldots(\sigma_{i_k}\xi)$.
  Hence,

$$\varphi^{-1}x^A\varphi = \varphi^{-1}\varphi(x\xi)^B = I_{sB}(x\xi)^B = (x\xi)^B.$$

Define the relation η between G_A and G_B by $x^A\eta = (x\xi)^B$. Since

$$x^A = y^A \Rightarrow \varphi^{-1}x^A\varphi = \varphi^{-1}y^A\varphi \Rightarrow (x\xi)^B = (y\xi)^B,$$

η is a *mapping* of G_A into G_B. Any element of G_B equals $(x\xi)^B$ for some $x \in (\Sigma^A)^*$ because ξ is a mapping of Σ^A onto Σ^B. Find in G_A the element y^A equal to x^A. Then $y^A\eta = (y\xi)^B = (x\xi)^B$ (because $y^A = x^A$), i.e., η is a mapping of G_A *onto* G_B. Finally,

$$(x^Ay^A)\eta = (xy)^A\eta = ((xy)\xi)^B = ((x\xi)(y\xi))^B = (x\xi)^B(y\xi)^B = (x^A\eta)(y^A\eta).$$

Hence, η is a homomorphism; thus, G_B is a homomorphic image of G_A.
  It may happen that the above η is an isomorphism without B being isomorphic to A. The following can serve as a simple example:

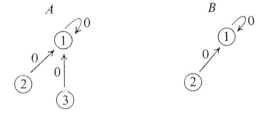

B is a homomorphic image of A with $\varphi = \begin{pmatrix} 1 & 2 & 3 \\ 1 & 2 & 2 \end{pmatrix}$ and $\xi = \begin{pmatrix} 0 \\ 0 \end{pmatrix}$.

$$G_A = \quad \wedge \quad 0 \quad = G_B.$$

	$\wedge$	0
$\wedge$	$\wedge$	0
0	0	0

A semiautomaton A, such that for every homomorphic (not iso-morphic) image B of it, the semigroup G_B is not isomorphic to G_A, can be considered as reduced in some sense.

Unfortunately, a semiautomaton A can have more than one such "reduced" homomorphic image with semigroups isomorphic to G_A.

EXAMPLE.

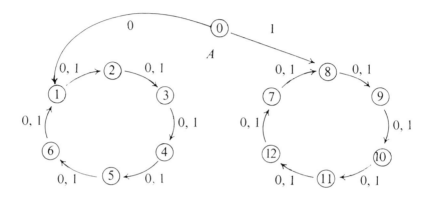

The following two semiautomata B and C are homomorphic images of A, both have semigroups isomorphic to G_A, and both are reduced in the above sense; but they are not isomorphic:

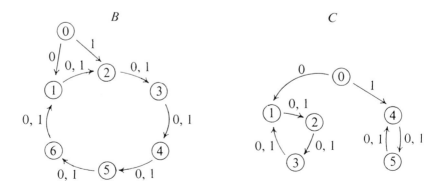

2.8 Nondeterministic Semiautomata

A *nondeterministic semiautomaton* is a triple $A = (S, \Sigma, M)$ in which S and Σ are as before and $M = \{\sigma^A\}_{\sigma \in \Sigma}$ with every σ^A a relation over S. For example:

$$A = \left(\{1, 2, 3, 4, 5\}, \{0, 1\}, \right.$$

$$\left\{ 0^A = \begin{pmatrix} 1 & 2 & 3 & 3 & 4 \\ 2 & 1 & 2 & 3 & 3 \end{pmatrix}, \quad 1^A = \begin{pmatrix} 1 & 3 & 4 & 4 & 4 \\ 4 & 4 & 2 & 3 & 5 \end{pmatrix} \right\} \right).$$

A deterministic semiautomaton is, thus, a nondeterministic one in which all the relations σ^A are mappings of S into S.

A nondeterministic semiautomaton can also be described by a directed graph; for the above example:

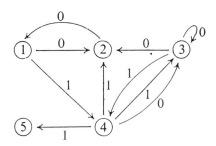

Notice that in this case there may be vertices from which no arrow emanates, and there may be vertices from which more than one arrow labeled by the same input emanate.

As before, the relation E over Σ^* defined by: $x \, E \, y \Leftrightarrow x^A = y^A$ (where $x^A = \sigma^A_{i_1} \sigma^A_{i_2} \ldots \sigma^A_{i_k}$ is the composition of the corresponding relations) is a congruence. The number of distinct relations over S is finite; hence, E has a finite index. Σ^*/E is a finite semigroup isomorphic to the semigroup G_A of relations generated by the relations $\{\sigma^A\}_{\sigma \in M} \cup \{M_\wedge\}$, which is called the semigroup of A.

One can use the congruence E and construct, as in Section 2.3, a deterministic cyclic semiautomaton corresponding to E. This construction puts in correspondence to every nondeterministic semiautomaton a deterministic one—a fact which will be used later.

The nondeterministic device can be considered as an adequate model for some actual situations, but its main importance is in providing a flexible tool to investigate automata. Many notions introduced before can be transferred to the new device, but as it plays an auxiliary role here, this will be done only if necessary in the appropriate place.

The reader should not confuse the nondeterministic semiautomaton with a probabilistic one. In the last, some distribution of probabilities is given for the event of passing from a state s to any $s_1 \in S$ when σ is applied, and the performance of the semiautomaton is studied mostly from the point of view of theory of probability.

Chapter 3

Recognizers (Rabin–Scott Automata)

3.1 Automata

A semiautomaton $A = (S, \Sigma, M)$ serves as a "skeleton" of an important device called *recognizer, Rabin-Scott Automaton*, or, simply, *Automaton* [37].

DEFINITION.   The quintuple $\hat{A} = (S, \Sigma, M, s_0, F)$, where S, Σ, M are as before, s_0 (the initial state) is a distinguished element of S, and F (the set of final states) is a distinguished subset of S, is called a (*finite*) *automaton*.

$\hat{A}$ is used to classify (or recognize) words in Σ^*. To this end let $\hat{A}$ be set in the state s_0 and a word $x \in \Sigma^*$ applied to it. If, after "reading" x, $\hat{A}$ is in a state belonging to F, it is said to *accept* the word x, otherwise x is rejected (not accepted) by $\hat{A}$.
   Formally:

DEFINITION.   The word $x \in \Sigma^*$ is accepted by $\hat{A}$ if and only if $s_0 x^A \in F$.
   $\hat{A}$ partitions Σ^* into two disjoint subsets: $U = T(\hat{A})$, the set of words accepted by $\hat{A}$, and $\Sigma^* - U$, the set of words rejected by $\hat{A}$. A set of words accepted by an automaton is called a *regular set*.
   $A = (S, \Sigma, M)$ is called the semiautomaton of the automaton $\hat{A} =$

55

(S, Σ, M, s_0, F). By changing the initial state and/or the set of final states, one can obtain various automata from the same semiautomaton A.

The states which can be reached from the initial state are the only ones relevant to the performance of an automaton $\hat{A}$. Hence, when an automaton $\hat{A}$ is discussed from the point of view of its recognition abilities, one can limit the consideration to the cyclic subsemiautomaton of A generated by s_0.

A nondeterministic semiautomaton A can serve as a skeleton of a *nondeterministic automaton* $\hat{A}$, which is defined similar to the deterministic one, with the difference that the initial state s_0 may be replaced by a set S_0 of initial states (S_0 is a subset of S).

$\hat{A}$ is said to accept a word $x \in \Sigma^*$ if and only if

$$S_0 x^A \cap F \neq \phi,$$

i.e., if there exists at least one path from an initial state to a final state along arrows labeled (in the appropriate order, of course) by the letters of x.

3.2   The Characterization of Regular Sets

A deterministic automaton is a special case of a nondeterministic one; hence, a set of tapes recognized by a deterministic automaton is recognized by a nondeterministic one. Now it will be shown that the opposite is also true.

Let $\hat{A} = (S, \Sigma, M, S_0, F)$ be a nondeterministic automaton. Consider the congruence E over Σ^* induced by the nondeterministic semiautomaton $A = (S, \Sigma, M)$ of $\hat{A}$. By definition

$$x\,E\,y \Leftrightarrow x^A = y^A,$$

hence, $x\,E\,y \Rightarrow (x \in U \Leftrightarrow y \in U)$, where U is the set of words accepted by $\hat{A}$. This proves that the words in U form complete congruence classes of E in Σ^*.

Now, if a (right) congruence E over Σ^* with a finite index is given, one can construct a deterministic automaton $\hat{A}'$ which will accept exactly a set of words U, provided that U is a union of complete congruence classes of E.

To this end a deterministic semiautomaton A' is constructed as in Section 2.3; the state corresponding to the congruence class containing $\wedge$ will be s_0'; F' is the set of states corresponding to the congruence classes consisting of elements of U. A word $x \in \Sigma^*$, applied to $\hat{A}'$ in s_0', will bring it to the state corresponding to the class containing $\wedge x = x$; i.e., x will be accepted by $\hat{A}'$ if and only if it belongs to U (then and only then the state corresponding to the congruence class of x is in F').

The above leads to the following two important theorems [37]:

THEOREM A.   A subset of Σ^* is a regular set if and only if it is a union of complete congruence classes of a (right) congruence with a finite index over Σ^*.

THEOREM B.   A set of words accepted by a nondeterministic automaton is a regular set; hence, a deterministic automaton can be constructed recognizing the set of words accepted by a given nondeterministic one.

The last theorem shows that there is no point in preferring nondeterministic automata over deterministic ones: both types can do exactly the same things. Nevertheless, the flexibility of the nondeterministic device allows one to use it conveniently to prove theorems and produce procedures.

3.3   Examples of Regular and Nonregular Sets

The first theorem in Section 3.2 characterizes regular sets as subsets of Σ^* which form complete congruence classes of right congruence relations with finite indexes over Σ^*. Thus, for example, every finite subset of Σ^* is a regular set. Indeed, let U be a finite subset of Σ^* and let h be the length of the longest word in U. Partition Σ^* as follows: every word of length smaller or equal to h forms a separate class, all other words together form a class. The corresponding equivalence relation E over Σ^* is a congruence (cf. 1.10). E has a finite index, and the words in U form complete congruence classes of E; hence, U is a regular set.

Let $\Sigma = \{0\}$. A cyclic automaton $\hat{A}$ with one input must have the following graph:

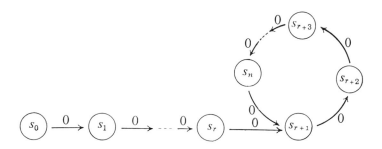

If no one of the states $s_{r+1}, s_{r+2}, \ldots, s_n$ belongs to F, then $\hat{A}$ will accept only a finite number of words. If $s_{r+i} \in F$, then $\hat{A}$ will accept all words of the form $0^{r+i}0^{(n-r)k}$, where $k = 0, 1, 2, \ldots$. Thus, $\hat{A}$ can accept only sets of words which are unions of a finite number of words and a finite number of infinite sequences of the above form, with a bounded "distance" between two consecutive words. But, for example, a sequence of words of the form:

$$0, 0^2, 0^4, 0^7, 0^{11}, 0^{16}, \ldots, 0^{\frac{1}{2}(k^2 - k + 2)}, \ldots$$

cannot be represented as such a union, because the distances between the consecutive words in it increase without bound. This is an example of a subset of Σ^* which is not regular. It was obtained by determining the sets of words which can be recognized by one input automata. Another approach is to directly use Theorem A in Section 3.2. So, one obtains the "classical" example of the set $U = \{0^k 10^k\}$ $(k = 1, 2, \ldots)$ over the two-letter alphabet $\Sigma = \{0, 1\}$. If U is regular, there must be at least two distinct words $0^{k_1}1$ and $0^{k_2}1$ $(k_1 \neq k_2)$ in one congruence class of the corresponding congruence relation (because it has a finite index).

Their right products by $0^{k_1} : 0^{k_1} 10^{k_1}$ and $0^{k_2} 10^{k_1}$ belong, consequently, to the same congruence class also, but this is impossible because the first is in U and the second is not.

3.4   Reduction and Homomorphism of an Automaton

Let $\hat{A} = (S, \Sigma, M, s_0, F)$ be an automaton and $E(s_0)$ the right congruence relation over Σ^* corresponding to the initial state s_0:

$$x \, E(s_0) \, y \Leftrightarrow s_0 x^A = s_0 y^A \qquad \text{(cf. 2.6)}.$$

The semiautomaton A of the automaton $\hat{A}$ is cyclic with s_0 as generator; hence, A is isomorphic to the semiautomaton A' corresponding to $E(s_0)$, and $|S|$ is equal to the index of $E(s_0)$. Every congruence class of $E(s_0)$ is composed of all words $x \in \Sigma^*$ such that $s_0 x^A$ is the same element of S. Hence, if $x \in T(\hat{A})$, i.e., $s_0 x^A \in F$, all other words in the congruence class of x will belong to $T(\hat{A})$ also. It follows that the words in $T(\hat{A})$ form complete congruence classes of $E(s_0)$.

Now let U be a regular set and E *any* right congruence over Σ^* with a finite index such that U is a union of congruence classes of E. Using E one constructs an automaton $\hat{A}$ which accepts the words in U and only them. The number of states of $\hat{A}$ is equal to the index of E, so it is natural to look for a right congruence satisfying the above conditions and having the smallest possible index.

DEFINITION.

$$x \, E_1 \, y \Leftrightarrow (\text{for every } t \in \Sigma^*, \quad xt \in U \Leftrightarrow yt \in U) \qquad (x, y \in \Sigma^*).$$

E_1 is an equivalence (reflexivity and symmetry are evident, and

$$x \, E_1 \, y, \, y \, E_1 \, z \Rightarrow (\text{for every } t, \quad xt \in U \Leftrightarrow yt \in U \Leftrightarrow zt \in U);$$

hence, $x \, E_1 \, z$ also). E_1 is even a right congruence, because

$$x \, E_1 \, y \Rightarrow (\text{for every } t, v \in \Sigma^*, \quad xtv \in U \Leftrightarrow ytv \in U)$$
$$\Rightarrow (\text{for every } v, \quad (xt)v \in U \Leftrightarrow (yt)v \in U)$$
$$\Rightarrow xt \, E_1 \, yt.$$

The elements of U form complete classes of E_1, because

$$x \, E_1 \, y \; \Rightarrow \; (x \in U \Leftrightarrow y \in U)$$

(take $t = \wedge$ in the definition of E_1). Any other right congruence relation E over Σ^* having this property is finer than E_1. Indeed, let $x \, E \, y$. Then, for any t in Σ^*, $xt \, E \, yt$; consequently, for every t, $xt \in U \Leftrightarrow yt \in U$, and so $x \, E_1 \, y$. So if $\hat{A}$ is an automaton accepting U, its $E(s_0) \subseteq E_1$, and as $|S|$ is equal to the index of $E(s_0)$, it follows that the automaton $\hat{A}_1 = (S^{A_1}, \Sigma, M^{A_1}, s_0^{A_1}, F^{A_1})$ constructed from E_1 has the smallest possible number of states among all automata recognizing U.

DEFINITION.   An automaton $\hat{B} = (S^B, \Sigma^B, M^B, s_0^B, F^B)$ is a *homomorphic image* of an automaton $\hat{A} = (S^A, \Sigma^A, M^A, s_0^A, F^A)$ if the semiautomaton B of $\hat{B}$ is a homomorphic image of the semiautomaton A of $\hat{A}$ and the corresponding mapping φ of S^A onto S^B satisfies:

$$s_0^A \varphi = s_0^B; \qquad s^A \in F^A \Leftrightarrow s^A \varphi \in F^B.$$

THEOREM.   The automaton $\hat{A}_1$ constructed above is a homomorphic image of any automaton $\hat{A} = (S^A, \Sigma, M^A, s_0^A, F^A)$ accepting U.

Proof.   It was noticed at the beginning of this section that A is isomorphic to the semiautomaton A' corresponding to the right congruence $E(s_0^A)$, hence one can consider A' instead of A. Since the states of A' are the congruence classes of $E(s_0^A)$, the states of A_1 are the congruence classes of E_1, and $E(s_0^A) \subseteq E_1$, it follows that the natural mapping φ which takes each congruence class of $E(s_0^A)$ onto the class of E_1 including it is a mapping of $S^{A'}$ onto S^{A_1}. The definition of φ implies that if the state (class) $s^{A'}$ includes $x \in \Sigma^*$ so does $s^{A'}\varphi$. Hence, for any $\sigma \in \Sigma$, both $s^{A'}\sigma^{A'}$ and $s^{A'}\varphi\sigma^{A_1}$ will include $x\sigma$, consequently, $s^{A'}\sigma^{A'}\varphi = s^{A'}\varphi\sigma^{A_1}$. This is true for every $s^{A'} \in S^{A'}$ and every $\sigma \in \Sigma$, hence φ is a homomorphic mapping of the semiautomaton A', i.e., also of A, onto the semiautomaton A_1.

Both states (classes) s_0^A (i.e., $s_0^{A'}$) and $s_0^{A_1}$ contain $\wedge$, hence $s_0^A\varphi = s_0^{A_1}$.
Finally,

$$s_0^A x^A \in F^A \Leftrightarrow x \in U \Leftrightarrow s_0^{A_1} x^{A_1} \in F^{A_1}.$$

But

$$s_{01}^A x^{A_1} = s_0^A \varphi x^{A_1} = s_0^A x^A \varphi,$$

hence

$$s_0^A x^A \in F^A \Leftrightarrow s_0^A x^A \varphi \in F^{A_1}.$$

Since any $s^A \in S^A$ can be written in the form $s_0^A x^A$ for some $x \in \Sigma^*$ it follows that

$$s^A \in F^A \Leftrightarrow s^A \varphi \in F^{A_1},$$

and all requirements in the definition of homomorphism are satisfied. Thus $\hat{A}_1$ is a homomorphic image of $\hat{A}$.

If an automaton $\hat{A}$ accepts U and has a minimal number of states, then the above homomorphism onto $\hat{A}_1$ must be an isomorphism. Hence $\hat{A}_1$ is the unique (up to renaming of states) minimal state automaton recognizing U.

A_1 is called *the reduced automaton* accepting U. A reduced automaton is one which has no proper homomorphic images, provided that its input set is held constant. Notice that every semiautomaton with more than one state has a proper homomorphic image: the one-state semiautomaton. On the other hand, because of the requirement.

$$s^A \in F^A \Leftrightarrow s^A \varphi \in F^B,$$

the corresponding automata may not have proper homomorphic images.

3.5   A Reduction Procedure

Let $\hat{A}$ be an automaton and $\hat{B}$ its homomorphic image with the same input set Σ. For any $x \in \Sigma^*$

$$x \in T(\hat{A}) \Leftrightarrow s_0^A x^A \in F^A \Leftrightarrow s_0^A x^A \varphi \in F^B \Leftrightarrow$$
$$s_0^A \varphi x^B \in F^B \Leftrightarrow s_0^B x^B \in F^B \Leftrightarrow x \in T(\hat{B}).$$

In words: the regular sets corresponding to an automaton and to its homomorphic image are equal. This result, together with Section 3.4, allows one to find the reduced automaton $\hat{A}_1$ corresponding to the given automaton $\hat{A}$ using the following procedure:

(1) If $\hat{A}$ has no proper homomorphic images with the same input set then $\hat{A}_1$ is isomorphic to $\hat{A}$ (i.e., one can take $\hat{A}$ as $\hat{A}_1$).
(2) Otherwise, let $\hat{B}$ be a proper homomorphic image of $\hat{A}$—call it $\hat{A}$ and return to (1).

Of course, it is desirable to find $\hat{A}_1$ in one step from $\hat{A}$ and, indeed, there are well-known procedures to this end [30, 35]. Nevertheless, in many cases it is simpler to perform the reduction by a multistep procedure in which every homomorphism is easily detectable.

In this connection, notice that a homomorphism of $\hat{A}$ can be obtained by determining an admissible partition of S^A, such that all states in the same block are final, or all of them do not belong to F^A.

A partition satisfying the last requirement is called *output consistent*.

THEOREM.   Every admissible output-consistent partition of S^A in $\hat{A}$ allows one to find a homomorphic image of $\hat{A}$; and, conversely, every homomorphic image of $\hat{A}$ induces such a partition.

Chapter 4

Regular Expressions

4.1 Definitions and the Basic Theorem

A regular set U can be described by a right congruence relation over Σ^*, or, equivalently, by an automaton accepting U.

A different approach uses the so-called *regular expressions*.

DEFINITION.   Given two sets of words R and S from Σ^* denote:

$R + S = \{x | x \in R \quad \text{or} \quad x \in S\}$ (the set theoretical union)

$R \cdot S = RS = \{xy | x \in R, y \in S\}$ (the multiplication, concatenation)

$R^* = \wedge + \{x | x$ is obtained by multiplying (concatenating) a finite number of words of $R\}$.

Notice that R^* denotes the set of words obtained as the union of all words in R^i for $i = 0, 1, 2, \ldots$, where $R^0 = \wedge$ and $R^i = (\ldots((RR)R)\ldots)R$ (i times).

Therefore, one also writes $R^* = \wedge + R + R^2 + \cdots$.

EXAMPLE.   Let $\Sigma = \{a, b\}$:

$R = \{a^2, ab\}$

$S = \{aba, ab, ba\}$

$$R + S = \{a^2, ab, aba, ba\}$$
$$RS = \{a^3ba, a^3b, a^2ba, ababa, abab, ab^2a\}$$
$$R^* = \{\wedge, a^2, ab, a^4, a^3b, aba^2, abab, a^6, \ldots\}.$$

$\{a^2, ab\}$ can be interpreted as $\{a^2\} + \{ab\}$. For a single word x no distinction will be made between the word itself and the set consisting of this word; i.e., x will be written instead of $\{x\}$. So, one writes

$$\Sigma = a + b, \qquad R = a^2 + ab, \qquad S = aba + ab + ba,$$

and so on. For the empty word $\wedge$ and any word $x \in \Sigma^*$, one has

$$\wedge x = x\wedge = x, \qquad \wedge\wedge = \wedge, \qquad \text{and} \qquad \wedge^* = \wedge.$$

The empty set (of words) ϕ is also considered and has to be carefully distinguished from the empty word $\wedge$. One has:

$$\phi + R = R, \qquad \phi R = R\phi = \phi, \qquad \phi^* = \wedge.$$

DEFINITION.   A *regular expression* is a formal expression obtained by a finite number of applications of operations from those listed in the previous definition to elements from the following list:

the characters of Σ,
the empty word $\wedge$,
the empty set ϕ,
and to expressions obtained from them by such applications of the above operations.

The precedence of the operations is (in decreasing order): $*, \cdot, +$, and brackets are used in the usual way.

So, for $\Sigma = \{a, b\}$:

$$b, a + ab, a^*, (a^2b + b)^*, \wedge, (\wedge + a)(a^2b^* + a)^*$$

are regular expressions.

Considering the letters of Σ, $\wedge$, and ϕ as sets of words in Σ^*, a regular expression can be interpreted as a finite sequence of applications of the above operations to subsets of Σ^*. Hence, *every regular expression represents a set of words from Σ^**. So b represents the word b, $a + ab$ represents the set of words $\{a, ab\}$, a^* the set $\{\wedge, a, a^2, a^3, \ldots\}$, and so on.

The following basic theorem belongs to Kleene [19]:

THEOREM.   The set of words $T(\hat{A})$ accepted by an automaton $\hat{A} = (S, \Sigma, M, s_0, F)$ can be represented by a regular expression over Σ, and, for every regular expression, there exists an automaton $\hat{A}$ such that $T(\hat{A})$ is equal to the set of words represented by this regular expression.

In other words, every regular set can be represented by a regular expression and every regular expression represents a regular set.

There are many proofs of this beautiful result. Before presenting one of them (in Section 4.6), the operations introduced in this section will be studied more carefully.

4.2   Properties of the Operations

The operations $+$, $\cdot$, and $*$ on subsets of Σ^* satisfy many identities. Those can be checked by applying the usual definition of equality of sets: two sets are equal if and only if they contain the same elements.

In the following list of basic identities, R, S, etc., will denote arbitrary (possibly also, not regular) sets of words from Σ^*, $\wedge$ is the empty word, ϕ the empty set. Some of the listed identities are obvious; others will be checked.

1. $R + R = R$, $R + \phi = R$

2. $R + S = S + R$

3. $(R + S) + T = R + (S + T)$

4. $(RS)T = R(ST)$ (Hence, this product can be written as RST.)

5. $R\wedge \; = \; \wedge R = R,$ $R\phi = \phi R = \phi$

6. $(R + S)T = RT + ST$

7. $T(R + S) = TR + TS$

8. $R^* R^* = R^*$

9. $(R^*)^* = R^*$

Indeed, $R^* \subseteq (R^*)^*$, and, on the other hand, $x \in (R^*)^*$ means $x = \wedge$ or x can be obtained by a concatenation of a finite number of words of R^*, hence, also of R; in both cases $x \in R^*$, and consequently, $(R^*)^* \subseteq R^*$.

10. $RR^* = R^* R$

11. $R^* = \wedge + R + R^2 + \ldots + R^k + R^{k+1} R^*$ $(\wedge^* = \wedge,$
    $\phi^* = \wedge)$

The right-hand side is, clearly, included in R^*. Now, $x \in R^*$ implies that $x = \wedge$ or $x \in R^i$ for some i. If $i \le k$, then R^i appears in the right-hand side. If $i > k$, then $R^i = R^{k+1} R^{i-k-1}$, and as $i - k - 1 \ge 0$, every word of R^{i-k-1} appears in R^*; hence, $x \in R^{k+1} R^*$. So R^* is included in the right-hand side of 11, which is thus established. A particular important case of 11 is:

12. $R^* = \wedge + RR^*$

Using the same reasoning as above one obtains for any function $F(R_1, \ldots, R_n)$, involving $+, \cdot, *$

13. $F(R_1, \ldots, R_n) + (R_1 + \cdots + R_n)^* = (R_1 + \cdots + R_n)^*$ that is

$$F(R_1, \ldots, R_n) \subseteq (R_1 + \cdots + R_n)^*$$

14. $(F(R_1^*, \ldots, R_n^*))^* = (R_1 + \cdots + R_n)^*$

Important particular case:

15. $(R^* + S^*)^* = (R^* S^*)^* = (R + S)^*$

16. $(RS)^* R = R(SR)^*$

Indeed, both sets consist of exactly those words which can be written in the form

$$r_1 s_1 r_2 s_2 \ldots r_k s_k r_{k+1} \quad (r_1, \ldots, r_{k+1} \in R, \quad s_1, \ldots, s_k \in S);$$

hence, they are equal.

The next identity will be obtained using previous ones instead of comparing the corresponding sets of words.

17. $(R^*S)^*R^* = (R + S)^*$

First compute the square of the left-hand side:

$$
\begin{aligned}
[(R^*S)^*R^*]^2 &= (R^*S)^*R^*(R^*S)^*R^* & \text{(by 12)} \\
&= (R^*S)^*R^*[\wedge + R^*S(R^*S)^*]R^* & \text{(by 6 and 7)} \\
&= (R^*S)^*R^*R^* + (R^*S)^*R^*R^*S(R^*S)^*R^* & \text{(by 8)} \\
&= (R^*S)^*R^* + (R^*S)^*R^*S(R^*S)^*R^* & \text{(by 6 and 7)} \\
&= (R^*S)^*[\wedge + R^*S(R^*S)^*]R^* & \text{(by 12)} \\
&= (R^*S)^*(R^*S)^*R^* & \text{(by 8)} \\
&= (R^*S)^*R^*.
\end{aligned}
$$

But $R^2 = R$ implies clearly that $R^* = R + \wedge$. Hence,

$$((R^*S)^*R^*)^* = (R^*S)^*R^* + \wedge = (R^*S)^*R^*.$$

On the other hand,

$$((R^*S)^*R^*)^* = (R^*S + R)^* = (S + RR^*S + R)^* = (S + R)^*$$

and the identity is proved. By 16: $R^*(SR^*)^* = (R + S)^*$.

18. $(R^*S)^* = (R + S)^*S + \wedge, \qquad (SR^*)^* = S(R + S)^* + \wedge$

These identities follow from the previous ones. Indeed, for example,

$$(R^*S)^* = (R^*S)^*R^*S + \wedge = (R + S)^*S + \wedge.$$

The last two will be inference rules:

19. $R = S^*T \Rightarrow R = SR + T$

Indeed,

$$R = S^*T = (SS^* + \wedge)T = SS^*T + T = SR + T.$$

20. (Arden) [2]: If $\wedge \notin S$, then $R = SR + T \Rightarrow R = S^*T$

$$R = SR + T \Rightarrow$$
$$R = S(SR + T) + T$$
$$= S^2R + ST + T$$
$$= S^2(SR + T) + ST + T$$
$$= S^3R + S^2T + ST + T = \cdots$$
$$= S^{k+1}R + (S^k + S^{k-1} + \cdots + S^2 + S + \wedge)T.$$

This is true for any k. Now, $\wedge \notin S$ implies that every word in the set $S^{k+1}R$ will be at least of length $k + 1$. If $x \in R$, then take $k = $ length of x and $x \notin S^{k+1}R$; i.e.,

$$x \in (S^k + S^{k-1} + \cdots + S^2 + S + \wedge)T$$

and, consequently, $x \in S^*T$. Conversely, if $x \in S^*T$, there must be an i such that $x \in S^iT$. Write $R = S^{i+1}R + (S^i + \cdots + S + \wedge)T$ and obtain $x \in R$. Thus, it is proved that $\wedge \notin S$ and $R = SR + T$ imply a unique solution $R = S^*T$. (For $S = \phi$, 20 reduces to $R = T \Rightarrow R = T$.)

4.3   Algebraic Manipulations with Regular Expressions

Two regular expressions are equal if and only if they represent equal subsets of Σ^*. One can try to prove such an equality by algebraic manipulations utilizing the identities of 4.2. There follow two examples. The corresponding expressions are over the two-letter alphabet $\Sigma = \{0, 1\}$.

(1) Prove:

$$(10)^*1 + (10)^*(11 + 0)[0 + 1(10)^*(11 + 0)]^*1(10)^*1$$
$$= [10 + (11 + 0)0^*1]^*1.$$

$(10)*1 + (10)*(11 + 0)[0+1(10)*(11 + 0)]*1(10)*1$ (by 17)

$= (10)*1 + (10)*(11 + 0)[0*1(10)*(11 + 0)]*0*1(10)*1$ (by 16)
$= (10)*1 + (10)*(11 + 0)0*1[(10)*(11 + 0)0*1]*(10)*1$ (by 6)
$= \{\wedge + (10)*(11 + 0)0*1[(10)*(11 + 0)0*1]*\}(10)*1$ (by 12)
$= [(10)*(11 + 0)0*1]*(10)*1$ (by 17)
$= [10 + (11 + 0)0*1]*1.$

This example is from reference [28]; the solution follows [9].

(2) Prove:

$[(1*0)*01*]* = \wedge + 0(0 + 1)* + (0 + 1)*00(0 + 1)*$ [27].
$[(1*0)*01*]*$ (by 18)

$= [((1 + 0)*0 + \wedge)01*]*$
$= [((1 + 0)*00 + 0)1*]*$ (by 18 from the left)
$= [(1 + 0)*00 + 0][(1 + 0)*00 + 0 + 1]* + \wedge$
$= [(1 + 0)*00 + 0](0 + 1)* \mid \wedge$
$= \wedge + 0(0 + 1)* + (0 + 1)*00(0 + 1)*.$

It will be shown later that the set of identities and the inference rules 19 and 20 introduced in Section 4.2 are complete in the sense that they enable proof of any equality of regular expressions. On the other hand, it is often very hard to prove in this way such equalities even with some experience. A description of a "mechanical" procedure for checking equalities follows [11].

4.4   Transition Graphs

Let $\Sigma = \{0, 1\}$ be a two-letter alphabet. (It is easy to see that there is no loss of generality in considering only a two-letter alphabet. This is not the case when one letter is taken. For example, in general, $RS \neq SR$, but in the one-letter case the product of sets of words is commutative.)

A *transition graph* over Σ is a finite directed graph in which every arrow is labeled by a 0 or a 1, or by a special symbol γ. At least one vertex of the graph is labeled by a $-$ sign (such vertices are called *initial*), and there may be vertices labeled by a + sign (*final* vertices). A vertex can be initial and final simultaneously. A word $x \in \Sigma^*$ is said to be accepted by the transition graph if there exists in it a path from an initial vertex to a final one such that the labels of the arrows along this path form the word x after deleting the γ's (if any). $\wedge$ is accepted by G if there is a vertex in G labeled both by $-$ and $+$, or if a γ-path leads from an initial vertex to a final one.

The set of words accepted by a transition graph G is denoted by $T(G)$.

EXAMPLES

1. Every nondeterministic automaton is a transition graph which doesn't have γ-arrows. The initial states are labeled $-$, the final $+$.

2. $T(G) = 1$

3. $T(G) = 1^*$

4. $T(G) = 11^*$

5. $T(G) = \phi$

6. $T(G) = \wedge$

7. $T(G) = 10^*$

8. $T(G) = (10^*)^*$

9. $T(G) = \wedge + 01 + 1$

THEOREM.   For every regular expression R there exists a transition graph G accepting exactly the set of words described by R. (Such a G is said to represent R.)

Proof.   This was done in the above examples for ϕ, $\wedge$, and the letters in Σ.

Let R and S be regular expressions and assume that they are represented by the transition graphs G and H, respectively. $R + S$ will be represented by the transition graph composed of G and H as two independent components. RS will be represented by the transition graph constructed in the following way: From every final vertex of G draw arrows to every initial vertex of H and label these arrows by γ. Erase the $+$ signs in the vertices of G and the $-$ signs in the vertices of H. The obtained combined graph has as initial vertices those which were initial in G, and as final ones those which were final in H.

R^* will be represented by the graph obtained from G in the following way: From every final vertex draw a γ-arrow to every initial vertex and, if necessary, add an isolated $\mp$ vertex to accept $\wedge$.

Every regular expression can be obtained from ϕ, $\wedge$, and the letters of Σ by a consecutive application of a finite number of $+$, $\cdot$, $*$ operations; hence, the theorem is proved by induction.

In practice one can often construct the graphs straightforward without using the above inductive steps.

EXAMPLES.

1. $R = [10 + (0 + 11)0^*1]^*1$

G_1:

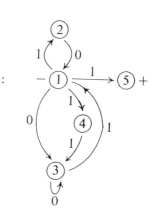

REMARK.   For later references the vertices of the transition graphs are numbered.

2. $R = [(1*0)*01*]*$

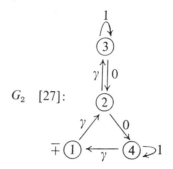

G_2 [27]:

3. $R = \wedge + 0(0 + 1)* + (0 + 1)*00(0 + 1)*$

G_3:

4.5   Sets of Words Corresponding to Transition Graphs

In this section will be proved the following theorem:

THEOREM.   The set of words $T(G) = T$ accepted by a transition graph G can be described by a regular expression effectively computable by the rules in Section 4.2.

First, some notions and constructions will be presented. For a set of words T and a word $x \in \Sigma^*$, denote by T_x—called *the derivative of T with respect to x* [5]—the set

$$T_x = \{y | xy \in T\}.$$

The graph G representing T can be used to represent any derivative T_x of T. To this end, denote by A_x the set of *all* vertices in G which can be reached from the initial vertices following a path corresponding to the word $x \in \Sigma^*$ (including any γ-arrows, of course).

REMARK. A_x can be found by computation with relations as shown in 4.8.

If now, the previous $-$ signs are erased and all vertices in A_x are supplied with $-$ signs, one will obtain a transition graph G' representing the set of words T_x. Indeed, it follows from the definition of T_x that it consists of all words, and only of those words, which correspond to paths leading from the vertices in A_x to the final vertices in G.

Thus, to every derivative T_x of T there corresponds a set A_x of vertices of G. The original initial vertices and all those which can be reached from them by a path of γ-arrows form $A_\wedge$ and correspond to $T_\wedge = T$. G has a finite number of vertices, hence a finite number of distinct subsets of vertices. It follows that any set of words T represented by a transition graph, in particular every set of words described by a regular expression, has a finite number of distinct derivatives. It is important to remark that the correspondence between the subsets of the set of vertices of G and the unequal derivatives of T is not one-to-one. To every derivative there corresponds at least one such subset, but there may be subsets to which no derivative corresponds, and there may also be distinct subsets corresponding to equal derivatives.

Given a transition graph G one constructs a corresponding *table of derivatives* of $T(G) = T$. This will be demonstrated for the graph G_1 in Section 4.4 by Table I.

The entries in the first column (Inputs) of Table I are words $x \in \Sigma^*$ ordered by length and for the same length by the numerical magnitude. In the second column (Vertices of G) the corresponding subsets of vertices A_x are marked. Thus,

$$A_\wedge = \{1\}, \qquad A_0 = \{3\}, \qquad A_1 = \{2, 4, 5\}, \qquad A_{00} = \{3\}, \qquad .$$

and so on, as can be read directly from the graph.

Table I

DERIVATIVES OF $T(G) = T^a$

Inputs	Vertices of G					Equal to	Includes ∧
	1	2	3	4	5+		
∧	✓					—	—
0		✓				—	—
1	✓		✓	✓		—	yes
00		✓				0	—
01	✓					∧	—
10	✓					∧	—
11		✓				0	—

^{a} For the graph G_1 in 4.4.

In the third column (Equal to), 0 appears in the row of 00 because $A_{00} = A_0$ (i.e., $T_{00} = T_0$). $A_{01} = A_\wedge$ implies ∧ in the row of 01, etc. A row (and the corresponding derivative) with an entry in the column "Equal to" will be called a *terminal*. In this particular case, all derivatives of "second order" are terminal; i.e., they are equal to derivatives of smaller orders and, clearly, so will be all "higher" derivatives. Thus, the table need not be prolonged. As a rule, *if the row of x is terminal, one does not enter in the table more inputs beginning with x.*

In the last column (Includes ∧) a "yes" appears if and only if the corresponding A_x includes a final vertex (these vertices are labeled with a +).

The first entry in the inputs column is ∧, and then for any x which is *not terminal* the rows $x0$ and $x1$ are added to the table. The process is stopped when there are no new nonterminal words, and it must stop because there is only a finite number of subsets in a finite set.

As a second example, the derivatives for the graph G_2 in Section 4.4 are given in Table II.

The set of nonterminal derivatives includes all distinct derivatives of T although some of them may be represented in this set more than once.

The next observation is that one can write for any set of words T (in Σ^* with $\Sigma = \{0, 1\}$):

$$T = 0T_0 + 1T_1 + \alpha,$$

Table II

DERIVATIVES OF $T(G) = T^a$

Inputs	Vertices of G				Equal to	Includes $\wedge$
	$1+$	2	3	4		
$\wedge$	✓	✓	✓		—	yes
0	✓	✓	✓	✓	—	yes
1			✓		—	—
00	✓	✓	✓	✓	0	yes
01	✓	✓	✓	✓	0	yes
10		✓	✓		—	—
11			✓		1	—
100	✓	✓	✓	✓	0	yes
101			✓		1	—

^{a} For the graph G_2 in 4.4.

where $\alpha = \wedge$ if $\wedge \in T$, and $\alpha = \phi$ otherwise. Indeed, $0T_0$ is the subset of T composed of all words in T beginning with a 0, $1T_1$ describes all words in T beginning with a 1. Together they give all nonempty words of T, and α takes care of the empty one.

The table of derivatives will now be used to construct a system of equations of the following form. Let T_x be any nonterminal derivative. As above, one writes

$$T_x = 0T_{x0} + 1T_{x1} + \alpha_x,$$

where $\alpha_x = \wedge$ if $\wedge \in T_x$, and $\alpha_x = \phi$ otherwise. (This can be determined from the last column of the table). Then any terminal derivative on the right-hand side of the equation is replaced by the equal nonterminal derivative appearing in the third column of the table.

This procedure is applied to all nonterminal derivatives and a system of equations in which they appear as unknowns is obtained. So, for example, Table I leads to the following system:

$$T = T_{\wedge} = 0T_0 + 1T_1$$
$$T_0 = 0T_{00} + 1T_{01} = 0T_0 + 1T$$
$$T_1 = 0T_{10} + 1T_{11} + \wedge = 0T + 1T_0 + \wedge.$$

And Table II leads to the system:

$$T = T_\wedge = 0T_0 + 1T_1 + \wedge$$
$$T_0 = 0T_{00} + 1T_{01} + \wedge = 0T_0 + 1T_0 + \wedge$$
$$T_1 = 0T_{10} + 1T_{11} = 0T_{10} + 1T_1$$
$$T_{10} = 0T_{100} + 1T_{101} = 0T_0 + 1T_1.$$

Each such system has a solution for T (and for all T_x's appearing in it). To show this start with the last equation. If it has the form $T_x = 0T_y + 1T_z + \alpha_x$, where $y \neq x \neq z$, substitute the right-hand side for T_x in all previous equations and get a system without T_x (of course, with one equation less). If it has the form $T_x = 0T_x + 1T_z + \alpha_x$, one uses inference rule 20 from Section 4.2 to obtain $T_x = 0*(1T_z + \alpha_x)$, and substitutes this expression for T_x in the other equations. The same is done if the equation has the form

$$T_x = 0T_y + 1T_x + \alpha_x \qquad \text{or} \qquad T_x = (0 + 1)T_x + \alpha_x.$$

Next, apply the same procedure to the second to the last equation and so on. Rule 20 can always be applied, if necessary, because after any substitution into an equation $T_x = 0T_y + 1T_z + \alpha_x$, the T_x which will appear at the right-hand side will be necessarily multiplied from left by an expression representing a set of words each of which starts with a 0 or 1, i.e., is distinct from $\wedge$.

The consecutive application of the procedure to the equations from the bottom to the top of the system will lead finally to one equation with T, and if T will appear in it also at the right-hand side, rule 20 can be once more applied to give the answer.

The above procedure will be now demonstrated in the previous examples. For the first:

The last equation is $T_1 = 0T + 1T_0 + \wedge$. One substitutes this and obtains:

$$T = 0T_0 + 1(0T + 1T_0 + \wedge)$$
$$= 10T + (0 + 11)T_0 + 1$$
$$T_0 = 0T_0 + 1T.$$

Now one solves the second equation for T_0:

$$T_0 = 0*1T,$$

and substitutes the result in the first equation:

$$T = 10T + (0 + 11)0*1T + 1$$
$$= [10 + (0 + 11)0*1]T + 1.$$

The solution for T is:

$$T = [10 + (0 + 11)0*1]*1.$$

Notice that the answer is identical with the regular expression which led to the corresponding graph G_1.

The second system:

$$T = 0T_0 + 1T_1 + \wedge$$
$$T_0 = (0 + 1)T_0 + \wedge$$
$$T_1 = 0(0T_0 + 1T_1) + 1T_1$$
$$= 0^2T_0 + (01 + 1)T_1.$$

The second equation includes only T_0, and one can obtain $T_0 = (0 + 1)*$ from it. After substituting one gets:

$$T_1 = 0^2(0 + 1)* + (01 + 1)T_1,$$

that is,

$$T_1 = (01 + 1)*0^2(0 + 1)*$$

and finally

$$T = 0(0 + 1)* + 1(01 + 1)*0^2(0 + 1)* + \wedge.$$

The answer here is far from being identical to the regular expression which led to G_2, but it can be checked that both represent the same set of words.

Two important facts concerning the solution of the above systems of equations emerge. The first is that given a system of the form discussed before one can always solve it, and the set of words represented by the answer is unique (notice that only transformations from 4.2 were used). Thus, two systems with identical equations (up to names of the variables, of course) will yield the same solutions for the corresponding variables.

The second fact is that the expressions for the unknowns are obtained from the letters of Σ, and $\wedge$, and ϕ using the three operations $+$, $\cdot$, $*$; i.e., they are regular expressions. This shows that $T(G)$ is a regular expression for any transition graph G, and, moreover, this expression can be computed. The theorem at the beginning of the section is, therefore, proved.

4.6   Proof of Kleene's Theorem

Every automaton $\hat{A}$ can be represented by a finite directed graph G with an initial state and a set of final states. But G is a transition graph, hence one can build for it the table of derivatives and using it obtain the corresponding system of equations for $T(\hat{A}) = T(G)$ and its derivatives. The system can be solved and $T(\hat{A})$ obtained in a form of a regular expression over Σ. Notice that the outlined procedure is constructive, and it may be remarked that very often this is the simplest way to compute $T(\hat{A})$ for a given $\hat{A}$.

Thus, for every $\hat{A}$, the regular set $T(\hat{A})$ can be described by a regular expression over Σ.

Conversely, let R be a regular expression over Σ. One constructs for it a transition graph, which is used to build the table of derivatives, and from it the system of equations. Now a new transition graph is built in the following way. Its vertices correspond to the nonterminal derivatives, i.e., to the unknowns in the equations. If the equation for T_x is

$$T_x = 0T_y + 1T_z + \alpha_x$$

an arrow labeled with a 0 is drawn from the vertex corresponding to T_x

to the vertex T_y, and an arrow labeled with a 1 to the vertex T_z. Finally, the vertex corresponding to $T_\wedge = T$ is labeled with a $-$ sign, and the vertices which correspond to the derivatives, including $\wedge$, with a $+$ sign. The obtained transition graph is a graph of an automaton: from every vertex emanates one arrow with a 0 and one with a 1; there are no γ-arrows; there is one initial state and a set of final states. For example, one obtains for the first system in Section 4.5

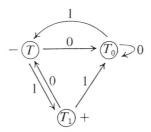

and for the second

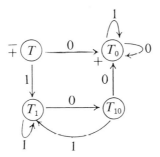

It is clear that the obtained transition graph will lead back exactly to the same table of derivatives; i.e., also to the same system of equations as that used to generate it. (Notice that for a graph of an automaton every A_x contains exactly one vertex.) It follows that $T(\hat{A})$ of the obtained automaton is equal to the given R, and, thus, it is proved that every regular expression is a regular set. The theorem of Kleene is proved in both directions.

The above construction provides a procedure to build an automaton corresponding to a given regular expression R. This procedure even gives the reduced automaton, if all derivatives involved are distinct. Indeed, to every derivative there corresponds one vertex, and if two derivatives have to be distinct, the corresponding vertices must be distinct, too. In other words, the number of vertices in an automaton $\hat{A}$ such that $T(\hat{A}) = R$ is at least equal to the number of distinct derivatives of R.

4.7   A Procedure for Checking Equality of Regular Expressions

The notions and techniques developed above provide a "mechanical" procedure for checking equality of regular expressions, which will now be described.

Let R and S be two regular expressions for which equality has to be checked. Start with constructing transition graphs corresponding to R and S and building the respective tables of derivatives. Using these tables one constructs the following "compound system of equations" for R and S. Beginning with the pair (the "column vector") $\begin{pmatrix} R \\ S \end{pmatrix}$, i.e. $\begin{pmatrix} R_\wedge \\ S_\wedge \end{pmatrix}$, one writes

$$\begin{pmatrix} R_\wedge \\ S_\wedge \end{pmatrix} = 0\begin{pmatrix} R_0 \\ S_0 \end{pmatrix} + 1\begin{pmatrix} R_1 \\ S_1 \end{pmatrix} + \begin{pmatrix} \alpha_\wedge \\ \beta_\wedge \end{pmatrix},$$

where $\alpha_\wedge$ (or $\beta_\wedge$) $= \wedge$, if R (or S, respectively) contains $\wedge$, and $= \phi$ otherwise. Using the tables of derivatives one replaces in the right-hand side of this equation the terminal derivatives of R and S by equal nonterminal derivatives as indicated in the "Equal to" columns of the tables.

Then for each pair $\begin{pmatrix} R_x \\ S_y \end{pmatrix}$ obtained in the right-hand side of the equation, one adds the equation

$$\begin{pmatrix} R_x \\ S_y \end{pmatrix} = 0\begin{pmatrix} R_{x0} \\ S_{y0} \end{pmatrix} + 1\begin{pmatrix} R_{x1} \\ S_{y1} \end{pmatrix} + \begin{pmatrix} \alpha_x \\ \beta_y \end{pmatrix}$$

(α_x and β_y have the usual meaning), and the terminal derivatives in the right-hand side are replaced by equal derivatives from the "Equal to" columns.

The procedure is continued until there are no new pairs of derivatives, i.e., until all pairs of derivatives appearing at the right-hand sides of the equations appear also at the left-hand sides. The number of distinct pairs will satisfy $u \leq n_R n_S$, where n_R and n_S are the numbers of non-terminal derivatives in the tables for R and S, respectively.

By enumerating the pairs, one obtains the compound system [40]

$$\binom{R_{(i)}}{S_{(i)}} = 0\binom{R_{(i_0)}}{S_{(i_0)}} + 1\binom{R_{(i_1)}}{S_{(i_1)}} + \binom{\alpha_{(i)}}{\beta_{(i)}}$$

where

$$i = 1, 2, \ldots, u, \quad 1 \leq i_0 \leq u, \quad 1 \leq i_1 \leq u, \quad R_{(1)} = R_\wedge, \quad S_{(1)} = S_\wedge,$$

and $\alpha_{(i)}$ and $\beta_{(i)}$ are $\wedge$ or ϕ. If $\alpha_{(i)} = \beta_{(i)}$ for every i, one has two identical systems of equations for the $R_{(i)}$'s and $S_{(i)}$'s; hence,

$$R_{(i)} = S_{(i)} \quad (i = 1, 2, \ldots, u);$$

particularly,

$$R = R_{(1)} = S_{(1)} = S.$$

Conversely, if $R = S$, then in the compound system one necessarily has $\alpha_{(i)} = \beta_{(i)}$ $(i = 1, 2, \ldots, u)$ because by the construction of the pairs the derivatives in every $\binom{R_{(i)}}{S_{(i)}}$ are equal to R_x and S_x correspondingly for some $x \in \Sigma^*$, and if $R = S$, then $R_x = S_x$ for every x.

Thus, the equality $R = S$ of two regular expressions holds if and only if in the above compound system for R and S, $\alpha_{(i)} = \beta_{(i)}$ for all i.

Of course, one does not need to write the equations explicitly; it is necessary only to find out all distinct pairs and check, using the "Includes $\wedge$" columns of the tables, if both elements in each pair simultaneously do or do not include $\wedge$.

EXAMPLE. It was proved in 4.3 that

$$\begin{aligned} R &\equiv [(1^*0)^*01^*]^* \\ &= \Lambda + 0(0 + 1)^* + (0 + 1)^*00(0 + 1)^* \\ &\equiv S. \end{aligned}$$

The transition graph and table of derivatives for R are given in Sections 4.4 and 4.5. The graph for S is G_3 in 4.4. Table III is the corresponding table of derivatives.

Table III

	Vertices of G				Equal	Includes
Inputs	1+	2	3	4+	to	Λ
Λ	√	√	√		—	yes
0		√	√	√	—	yes
1		√			—	—
00		√	√	√	0	yes
01		√		√	—	yes
10		√	√		—	—
11		√			1	—
010		√	√	√	0	yes
011		√		√	01	yes
100		√	√	√	0	yes
101		√			1	—

Now one looks for the pairs:

The pair $\binom{\Lambda}{\Lambda}$ implies

$$\binom{0}{0} \quad \text{and} \quad \binom{1}{1}.$$

The pair $\binom{0}{0}$ implies

$$\binom{00}{00} = \binom{0}{0} \quad \text{and} \quad \binom{01}{01} = \binom{0}{01}.$$

The pair $\begin{pmatrix} 1 \\ 1 \end{pmatrix}$ implies

$$\begin{pmatrix} 10 \\ 10 \end{pmatrix} \quad \text{and} \quad \begin{pmatrix} 11 \\ 11 \end{pmatrix} = \begin{pmatrix} 1 \\ 1 \end{pmatrix}.$$

The two added pairs $\begin{pmatrix} 0 \\ 01 \end{pmatrix}$ and $\begin{pmatrix} 10 \\ 10 \end{pmatrix}$ do not imply new ones; for example, $\begin{pmatrix} 0 \\ 01 \end{pmatrix}$ implies

$$\begin{pmatrix} 00 \\ 010 \end{pmatrix} = \begin{pmatrix} 0 \\ 0 \end{pmatrix} \quad \text{and} \quad \begin{pmatrix} 01 \\ 011 \end{pmatrix} = \begin{pmatrix} 0 \\ 01 \end{pmatrix}.$$

So the set of all appearing pairs is

$$\begin{pmatrix} \wedge \\ \wedge \end{pmatrix}, \quad \begin{pmatrix} 0 \\ 0 \end{pmatrix}, \quad \begin{pmatrix} 1 \\ 1 \end{pmatrix}, \quad \begin{pmatrix} 0 \\ 01 \end{pmatrix}, \quad \begin{pmatrix} 10 \\ 10 \end{pmatrix}.$$

$R = S$ because both elements in the pairs

$$\begin{pmatrix} \wedge \\ \wedge \end{pmatrix}, \quad \begin{pmatrix} 0 \\ 0 \end{pmatrix}, \quad \begin{pmatrix} 0 \\ 01 \end{pmatrix}$$

include $\wedge$, and both elements in the pairs

$$\begin{pmatrix} 1 \\ 1 \end{pmatrix}, \quad \begin{pmatrix} 10 \\ 10 \end{pmatrix}$$

do not include $\wedge$.

4.8   Computation of A_x

The use of the tables in the above procedure can be replaced by the following relational technique.

A transition graph G can be described by a set of relations over its vertex set in the obvious way: to every input $\sigma \in \Sigma$ and to γ there corresponds a relation F_σ such that $a\, F_\sigma\, b$ if and only if there is in G a σ-arrow from the vertex a to the vertex b.

Let $\bar{F}_\gamma$ be the transitive closure of the union $F_\gamma \cup I$ (I the identity relation). Then for any $x = \sigma_1 \sigma_2 \ldots \sigma_k \in \Sigma^*$, one has

$$A_x = A\bar{F}_\gamma F_{\sigma_1} \bar{F}_\gamma F_{\sigma_2} \bar{F}_\gamma \ldots \bar{F}_\gamma F_{\sigma_k} \bar{F}_\gamma, \qquad A_\wedge = A\bar{F}_\gamma,$$

where A is the set of the initial vertices of the transition graph G. Notice that $\bar{F}_\gamma$ can be obtained by multiplying $F_\gamma \cup I$ by itself, at most $n - 1$ times, where n is the number of vertices of G (cf. 1.7).

For example, for G_2 in 4.4 one has:

$$F_0 = \begin{pmatrix} 2 & 3 \\ 4 & 2 \end{pmatrix}, \qquad F_1 = \begin{pmatrix} 3 & 4 \\ 3 & 4 \end{pmatrix}, \qquad F_\gamma = \begin{pmatrix} 1 & 2 & 4 \\ 2 & 3 & 1 \end{pmatrix}$$

$$\bar{F}_\gamma = \begin{pmatrix} 1 & 2 & 3 & 4 & 1 & 2 & 4 & 1 & 4 & 4 \\ 1 & 2 & 3 & 4 & 2 & 3 & 1 & 3 & 2 & 3 \end{pmatrix}. \qquad A = \{1\}.$$

$$A_\wedge = \{1\}\bar{F}_\gamma = \{1, 2, 3\}.$$

$$A_{10} = A\bar{F}_\gamma F_1 \bar{F}_\gamma F_0 \bar{F}_\gamma = \{2, 3\},$$

and so on.

This computational approach may be utilized on a computer.

4.9   Axiomatic Approach to Regular Expressions

Regular expressions were obtained formally by recursive application of the operations $+$, $\cdot$, $*$ to the generators: the letters of Σ, and $\wedge$, and ϕ.

At the same time, the rules of manipulations with regular expressions were deduced from their interpretation as subsets of Σ^*. It is natural to seek an axiomatic definition of this system similar to those known for other algebraic systems (cf. Chapter 1). To this end a list of axioms fulfilled by the operations has to be provided. Applying the standard logical rules of inference (e.g., substitutivity of equality) and sometimes also special additional rules, which become in some sense a part of the system of axioms, one derives theorems from the axioms. One also looks for a concrete model of a (mathematical) structure satisfying the given set of axioms. For the considered case the regular sets in Σ^* serve naturally as such a model. Thus, to every expression in the algebra of regular expressions there corresponds the *unique* set of words described by it, according to the interpretations discussed earlier in this chapter. It is possible that to two nonidentical expressions R and S there correspond the same sets of words. In this case one would like to be able to prove this equality without using the interpretation. In other words, one would like to be able, by applying to R and S the axioms and theorems of the algebra (using the rules of inference, of course), to transform them into identical expressions (which will prove their equality). The system of axioms is called *complete* (with respect to the particular interpretation) if it allows one to reduce to identities all such equalities (equalities in the given interpretation).

In the next section will be proved the result by Redko [38] that there does not exist a finite complete set of axioms for the algebra of regular expressions with respect to their interpretation as regular sets, if the only rules of inference are the standard logical rules.

On the other hand, if rule 20 from 4.2 is added, such a finite complete system of axioms can be constructed.

4.10 The Nonsufficiency of a Finite System of Axioms

The alphabet Σ will consist of one letter σ.

$a, b, c, \ldots$ are arbitrary expressions which can be obtained from $\sigma, \wedge, \phi$ by recursive application of the operations $+, \cdot, *$ a finite number of times.

The set of axioms:

1. $a + b = b + a$
2. $a + (b + c) = (a + b) + c$

3. $a + a = a, \qquad a + \phi = a$

4. $ab = ba$

5. $(ab)c = a(bc)$

6. $a\wedge = a, \qquad a\phi = \phi$

7. $(a + b)c = ac + bc$

8. $\wedge^* = \wedge, \qquad \phi^* = \wedge$

9. $(ab^*)^* = \wedge + aa^*b^*$

10. $(a + b)^* = a^*b^*$

11_k. $a^* = (a^k)^*(\wedge + a + \cdots + a^{k-1}) \qquad k = 1, 2, \ldots.$

If a regular expression is interpreted as a set of words from $\Sigma^* = \sigma^*$ one can easily check that all above axioms hold in this model. Indeed 1, 2, 3, 5, 6, 7, 8 appear in 4.2; 4 holds because Σ has only one letter, and for any two words $u, v \in \sigma^*$ one has $uv = vu$. In 10, $(a + b)^*$ consists of all possible words generated by a and b. By commutativity in every product of words from a and b, those from a can be written at the beginning followed by the words from b. Hence, such a product will necessarily appear in a^*b^*. The inclusion in the other direction is obvious; hence, axiom 10 holds in the above model. 9 follows from rule 18 in Section 4.2, and axiom 10. Indeed,

$$(ab^*)^* = \wedge + a(a + b)^* = \wedge + aa^*b^*.$$

Finally, 11_k. Every word of a^* has the form $x = a_1 a_2 \ldots a_t$ where $a_1, a_2, \ldots, a_t$ are words of a. One writes

$$x = (a_1 \ldots a_k)(a_{k+1} \ldots a_{2k}) \ldots (a_{(s-1)k+1} \ldots a_{sk})(a_{sk+1} \ldots a_{sk+r})$$

where $r < k$. The product of the first s brackets belongs to $(a^k)^*$ and $a_{sk+1} \ldots a_{sk+r}$ is a word of a^r (and $r < k$). Hence, x belongs to the right-hand side expression. The opposite inclusion is evident, so axiom 11_k holds, too, in the above model, for every k.

Now it will be proved that the system is complete with respect to that interpretation. In other words, it will be shown that any equality $R = S$ ($R = S$ means here that the same regular sets correspond to R and S)

can be brought to an identity using the axioms 1–11, and the standard logical rules of inference.

If there are stars in R one can use the first ten axioms in order to have every star applied only to a single nonempty word. Let m be the least common multiple of the lengths of all words to which $*$ is applied in the obtained expression. If σ^i is one such word one uses 11 and writes: $(\sigma^i)^* = (\sigma^m)^*(\wedge + \sigma^i + \sigma^{2i} + \cdots + \sigma^{i(m/i - 1)})$ (notice: $k = m/i$). So, the $*$ is applied only to σ^m. One uses the equality $a^*a^* = (a + a)^* = a^*$ and the axioms 1–8, and transforms the expression to the form

$$(\sigma^m)^*a + b$$

where a and b are finite sums of distinct words.

Before proceeding, the following identities will be derived from the axioms:

$$a^* = (a\wedge)^* = (a\wedge^*)^* = \wedge + aa^*\wedge^* = \wedge + aa^*.$$

Hence,

$$a^* + \wedge = \wedge + aa^* + \wedge = \wedge + aa^* = a^*.$$

One obtains, also, as in 4.2

$$a^* = \wedge + aa^*$$
$$= \wedge + a(\wedge + aa^*)$$
$$= \wedge + a + a^2a^*$$
$$\cdots$$
$$= \wedge + a + a^2 + \cdots + a^ka^* \qquad (k = 1, 2, \ldots).$$

Every word in a and b in the expression $(\sigma^m)^*a + b$ has the form σ^t. Let

$$b = \sigma^{t_1} + \sigma^{t_2} + \cdots + \sigma^{t_r},$$

and denote:

$$t = \max(t_1, t_2, \ldots, t_r).$$

Let k be such that $km > t$. Write:

$$(\sigma^m)^*a + b = (\wedge + \sigma^m + \sigma^{2m} + \cdots + \sigma^{(k-1)m})a$$
$$+ \sigma^{km}(\sigma^m)^*a + \sigma^{t_1} + \sigma^{t_2} + \cdots + \sigma^{t_r}.$$

Compare the words of $(\wedge + \sigma^m + \cdots + \sigma^{(k-1)m})a$ with the words of b, and if some word σ^{t_i} appears in both use axiom 3 and delete it from b. After this is done the expression is transformed to $(\sigma^m)^*a + b'$, where b' is the sum of the remaining words of b. Moreover, it is clear that no word of $(\sigma^m)^*a$ is equal to a word of b'.

Next, if a word $\sigma^r \in b'$ and $\sigma^{r+m} \in a$ then

$$(\sigma^m)^*\sigma^{r+m} + \sigma^r = ((\sigma^m)^*\sigma^m + \wedge)\sigma^r = (\sigma^m)^*\sigma^r.$$

Perform consecutively all such possible transformations and get the expression $(\sigma^m)^*a' + b''$ in which

$$\sigma^r \in b'' \Rightarrow \sigma^{r+m} \notin a'.$$

Finally, turn to a' and assume that

$$a' = \sigma^{s_1} + \sigma^{s_2} + \cdots + \sigma^{s_p}.$$

For every i write $s_i = u_i m + v_i$, where $v_i < m$. Assume that $v_i = v_j$ and $u_i < u_j$. Then:

$$(\sigma^m)^*\sigma^{u_i m + v_i} + (\sigma^m)^*\sigma^{u_j m + v_i}$$
$$= ((\sigma^m)^* + (\sigma^m)^*\sigma^{(u_j - u_i)m})\sigma^{u_i m + v_i}$$
$$= [\wedge + \sigma^m + \sigma^{2m} + \cdots + \sigma^{(u_j - u_i)m}(\sigma^m)^*$$
$$+ (\sigma^m)^*\sigma^{(u_j - u_i)m}]\sigma^{u_i m + v_i}$$
$$= [\wedge + \sigma^m + \sigma^{2m} + \cdots + \sigma^{(u_j - u_i)m}(\sigma^m)^*]\sigma^{u_i m + v_i}$$
$$= (\sigma^m)^*\sigma^{u_i m + v_i}.$$

It follows that σ^{s_j} can be deleted from a'. This has to be done consecutively for all equalities $v_i = v_j$. The obtained set of words will be denoted by a'' and R is thus transformed to the form $(\sigma^m)^*a'' + b''$, which will be called reduced.

Let $R = S$. First change R and S so that in both the $*$ will be applied to single words only, and let m be the least common multiple of the lengths of those words at both sides. Transform R and S to the reduced form (with the same m for both; notice that the reductions were done without any reference to the origin of m). One gets:

$$(\sigma^m)^*a_1 + b_1 = (\sigma^m)^*a_2 + b_2.$$

The claim is that if both sides represent the same sets of words, they are identical. Let σ^u be a word of b_1. If it appears in $(\sigma^m)^*a_2$, then there exists in a_2 a word σ^r such that $km + r = u$ for some nonnegative integer k. Hence, at the right-hand side appear the words

$$(\sigma^m)^*\sigma^r = \sigma^r + \sigma^{m+r} + \sigma^{2m+r} + \cdots + \sigma^{km+r} + \sigma^{(k+1)m+r}(\sigma^m)^*.$$

All words $(\sigma^m)^*\sigma^r$ must appear also at the left-hand side and by the reduction procedure they must be a part of $(\sigma^m)^*a_1$. But then $\sigma^u = \sigma^{km+r}$ is also included in $(\sigma^m)^*a_1$, and, thus, it cannot appear in b_1. Hence, every word of b_1 must appear in b_2, and by symmetry every word of b_2 appears in b_1. Thus, $b_1 = b_2$ identically. Now let $\sigma^r \in a_1$. The set of words $(\sigma^m)^*\sigma^r$ must belong to $(\sigma^m)^*a_2$. Hence, there exists a word $\sigma^s \in a_2$ such that $r = km + s$. Now all words $\sigma^s, \sigma^{m+s}, \ldots, \sigma^{(k-1)m+s}$ appear at the right-hand side and not in b_2 (because they appear in $(\sigma^m)^*a_2$). Hence, they do not appear in b_1, but in $(\sigma^m)^*a_1$. This means, however, that a_1 includes a word σ^u such that $s = hm + u$. Then

$$r = km + hm + u = (k + h)m + u,$$

and by the reduction procedure σ^r and σ^u cannot both belong to a_1. It follows that $k = h = 0$, i.e., $\sigma^r \in a_2$, and, consequently, $a_1 = a_2$ identically.

The completeness of the axiom system is thus proved.

Denote this axiom system by A. Assume that there exists a finite complete axiom system A_1 for the regular expressions over σ. A is complete; hence, the axioms of A_1 can be obtained from A, each one in a finite number of steps.[†] But in such derivation of A_1, only a finite number of axioms of A can take part; hence, there exists in A a finite subset A_2 of axioms such that it allows the derivation of A_1, and as A_1 is complete,

---

[†] Professor Arto Salomaa pointed out to the author that this assertion follows from the above argument only in the case when the axioms in A_1 involve one letter only.

A_2 will be complete, too. Thus, if there exists a finite complete axiom system for the regular expressions over σ, then A must contain a finite complete subsystem A_2. The final step in the development will be to show that A has no such a complete finite subsystem. This will be established by proving that the instance of axiom 11_p:

$$\sigma^* = (\sigma^p)^*(\wedge + \sigma + \cdots + \sigma^{p-1})$$

for a fixed prime p cannot be obtained from axioms 1–10 and the axioms 11 in which k is any positive integer except those which are divisible by p. Denote by A' this subsystem of A containing all axioms of A but those axioms 11 in which $k = sp$, $s = 1, 2, \ldots$.

DEFINITION.   The star-height $h(R)$ of a regular expression R is a nonnegative integer defined as follows [8]:

$$h(\sigma) = h(\wedge) = h(\phi) = 0 \qquad (\sigma \in \Sigma)$$
$$h(R_1 + R_2) = h(R_1 R_2) = \max\{h(R_1), h(R_2)\}$$
$$h(R^*) = h(R) + 1.$$

In other words, the star-height can be defined as the maximal number of nested stars in the expression. For example, $[(0 + 1)1^* + (0^*1)^*]^*0^*$ has the star-height 3.

Let V be a regular expression having a nonzero star-height; $\psi(V)$ will be the set of integers defined as follows: if V has star-height 1 then $\psi(V)$ is the set of integers showing the lengths of all words distinct from $\wedge$ under the star operation in V. If V has the star-height n, then $\psi(V)$ will be the union of the set of integers showing the lengths of all words in V distinct from $\wedge$ and nested into n stars, and the set $\psi(V')$, where V' is obtained from V by replacing all those words by $\wedge$.

EXAMPLE. $V = ((\sigma^2(\wedge + \sigma))^*(\sigma^4)^*)^* + (\sigma^5 + \sigma^4(\sigma^3 + \wedge)^*)^*\sigma + \wedge$.

The words not equal to $\wedge$ "under 2 stars" are σ^2, σ^3, σ^4, and σ^5. $\psi(V) = \{2, 3, 4\} \cup \psi(V')$ where V' is obtained by replacing those words by $\wedge : V' = \wedge + (\sigma^5 + \sigma^4)^*\sigma + \wedge = (\sigma^5 + \sigma^4)^*\sigma + \wedge$. Now one looks for words under one star—these are σ^5 and σ^4. Hence, $\psi(V') = \{4, 5\}$ and $\psi(V) = \{2, 3, 4, 5\}$.

Let V be a regular expression for which at least one number in the set $\psi(V)$ is not divisible by p. Apply to V one of the axioms in A' and obtain U. Then, also, $\psi(U)$ contains a number not divisible by p. Indeed, application of an axiom means replacing in V an instance of one side of that axiom by its other side. The above assertion is surely true when one of the axioms 1–8, or 10, is applied. For 9 and 11' (11' are all axioms 11 in which p does not divide k) this can be shown as follows.

Let $\overline{V}$ be the instance in V of such an axiom which is replaced by the other side $\overline{V}'$ of this axiom. If $\psi(\overline{V})$ contains a number not divisible by p then the application of 9 or 11' (in both possible directions) will preserve this property. This is true because:

(i) for any subexpression $\overline{V}$ of V, $\psi(\overline{V}) \subseteq \psi(V)$

(ii) $\psi((ab^*)^*) = \psi(\wedge + aa^*b^*)$

(iii) if there is a number not divisible by p in one of the two sets $\psi(a^*)$ or $\psi((a^k)^*(\wedge + a + \cdots + a^{k-1}))$ then such a number appears also in the other set (remember that k is not a multiple of p).

Assume now that all numbers in $\psi(\overline{V})$ are divisible by p. Let q be a number in $\psi(V)$ not divisible by p, i.e., there exists a word x of length q in V (but not in $\overline{V}$) under the star operation. If replacing $\overline{V}$ by $\overline{V}'$ does not involve in any way the word x then it will appear also in U under the star operation and $q \in \psi(U)$. Now, the transformation $\overline{V} \to \overline{V}'$ may possibly affect q (by implying changes involving x) only in the following cases:

(i) $x(ab^*)^*$ or xa^* are under the star operation in V and they are replaced by $x(\wedge + aa^*b^*)$ or $x(a^k)^*(\wedge + a + \cdots + a^{k-1})$, respectively, under the star operation in U. In either case x will appear under the star operation in U, hence $q \in \psi(U)$.

(ii) x is a product of a word y by a word from $\wedge + aa^*b^*$ or $\wedge + a + \cdots + a^{k-1}$, $y + yaa^*b^*$ or $(a^k)^*(y + ya + \cdots + ya^{k-1})$ appear under the star operation in V, and these expressions are replaced by $y(ab^*)^*$ or ya^*, respectively, under the star operation in U. Since the length of any word in a is divisible by p [otherwise $\psi(\overline{V})$ would contain numbers not divisible by p], the length of y is $q - m$ where m is a multiple of p, and $\psi(U)$ contains the number $q - m$ which is not divisible by p.

EXAMPLES.

$$V = (\sigma^6(\wedge + \sigma^5(\sigma^5)^*(\sigma^{10})^*))^* = (\sigma^6(\sigma^5(\sigma^{10})^*)^*)^* = U$$

$$p = 5; \quad \psi(V) = \{5, 10, 6, 11\}, \quad \psi(U) = \{10, 5, 6\} \quad\quad (11 - 5 = 6)$$

$$V = ((\sigma^{12})^*(\wedge + \sigma^3 + \sigma^6 + \sigma^9)\sigma^4)^* = ((\sigma^3)^*\sigma^4)^* = U$$

$$p = 3; \quad k = 4; \quad \psi(V) = \{12, 4, 7, 10, 13\}, \quad \psi(U) = \{3, 4\}$$
$$(7 - 3 = 10 - 2 \cdot 3 = 13 - 3 \cdot 3 = 4).$$

Thus, $\psi(U)$ contains a number not divisible by p if $\psi(V)$ contains such a number. The same property will hold for any transformation of V by the axioms because any such transformation is a chain of one-step transformations involving one axiom at a time.

Now, in $\sigma^* = (\sigma^p)^*(\wedge + \sigma + \cdots + \sigma^{p-1})$

$$\psi(\sigma^*) = \{1\} \quad\quad \text{and} \quad\quad \psi[(\sigma^p)^*(\wedge + \sigma + \cdots + \sigma^{p-1})] = \{p\}.$$

p does not divide 1, but p divides p; hence, it is impossible to get the right-hand side from the left-hand side by applying the axioms A'.

Consequently, an axiom subsystem will not be complete without axioms of the form 11_{ps} for every prime number p. Hence, infinitely many axioms are needed, and altogether one obtains the following theorem:

THEOREM [38].   There does not exist a finite complete system of axioms in the algebra of regular expressions over an alphabet with one letter (provided only the standard logical rules of inference are used)[†].

It follows that the same holds for an algebra of regular expressions over any alphabet. Indeed, if a complete finite system would exist for some alphabet the reduction of the system to a one-letter alphabet would be a finite complete system of axioms for the regular expressions over a one-letter alphabet, which is impossible.

4.11   A Complete Finite Axiom System

The addition of the rule of inference 20 from 4.2:

$$a = ba + c, \ \wedge \notin b \Rightarrow a = b^*c$$

---

† This has been proved here only for axioms which can be derived from the system A, in particular for any axiom involving one letter only (cf. the footnote on p. 89).

enables the construction of a finite complete set of axioms for the algebra of regular expressions.

The following system belongs to Salomaa [40] (cf. also reference [1]):

$$a + (b + c) = (a + b) + c$$

$$a(bc) = (ab)c$$

$$a + b = b + a$$

$$a(b + c) = ab + ac$$

$$(a + b)c = ac + bc$$

$$a + a = a$$

$$a\phi^* = a$$

$$a\phi = \phi$$

$$a + \phi = a$$

$$a^* = \phi^* + aa^*$$

$$a^* = (\phi^* + a)^*, \qquad \phi^* = \wedge .$$

In order to be able to apply the above rule of inference, the meaning of $\wedge \in a$ must be defined. This is done in the following way:

$\wedge \in a$ if and only if:

(1) $a = \wedge$,

(2) $a = b^*$ for some b

(3) $a = b_1 + \cdots + b_k$ where $\wedge \in b_i$ for some i

(4) $a = b_1 b_2 \ldots b_k$ where $\wedge \in b_i$ for all i.

The proof that the above system is complete is actually provided in 4.7. Using those techniques (without relying on the interpretation of the derivatives) one constructs for R and S the compound system of equations. The introduced rule of inference allows one to solve it for R and S. The results will be identical if and only if the same subsets of Σ^* correspond to R and S; i.e., if $R = S$ in the underlying model for the regular expressions.

4.12   Closure Properties of Regular Sets. A Canonical Form of a Regular Expression

The regular sets were shown to form a closed system under the operations of $+$, $\cdot$ and $*$.

The complement $T' = \Sigma^* - T$ of a regular set T is regular too. Indeed, consider the congruence E (over Σ^*) with finite index, corresponding to T according to Theorem A in 3.2. T' is a union of those complete congruence classes of E, which do not contain the elements of T, hence T' is a regular set by the same theorem.

For any two subsets of Σ^*, T_1 and T_2 one has $T_1 \cap T_2 = (T_1' \cup T_2')'$. It follows that if T_1 and T_2 are regular sets so will be $T_1 \cap T_2$.

ϕ and Σ^* are clearly regular sets, and the regular sets form a Boolean algebra of sets under the operations $+$, $\cap$ and $'$.

Let $x \in \Sigma^*$. Denote by x^R the word obtained from x by reading it backwards (from right to left). For example,

$$01^R = 10, \qquad 10011^R = 11001, \qquad 1^R = 1, \qquad \wedge^R = \wedge, \qquad \text{etc.}$$

Change in the transition graph corresponding to a regular set T the directions of all arrows and denote by $+$ the vertices with $-$ signs and vice versa (i.e., the previous initial vertices will now be final and the previous final vertices will now be initial). The obtained transition graph describes the set $T^R = \{x^R | x \in T\}$ which is thus a regular set.

It follows from 4.5 that a derivative of a regular set is a regular set too.

There are also known various additional operations with regular sets preserving the "regularity."

Every regular expression can be uniquely represented by the reduced automaton accepting the corresponding regular set. In this sense one can consider the reduced automaton as a *canonical form* of the regular expression. Nevertheless, one would like to have an algebraic canonical form. This problem is still not solved in its general setting and appears to be rather difficult. For particular classes of regular expressions there exist such canonical forms. The reduced form of a regular expression over a one-letter alphabet introduced in 4.10 provides one example. Others can be found in [4, 34, 45].

Chapter 5

Coverings of Automata

5.1 Moore and Mealy Machines

The automaton defined in Section 3.1 can be interpreted as a machine with two outputs, say 0 and 1. The output depends on the state to which the device is transformed by the corresponding input: if this is a final state the output is 1, otherwise 0.

In the same way one can consider an automaton with a set Θ of outputs and a mapping N from S into Θ, which attaches to some (possibly to all) states of S outputs from Θ. The corresponding device is called a *Moore machine* [30]. The next step is to make the outputs depend not only on the states of $\hat{A}$, but also on the inputs. In other words, one obtains a set of mappings N_σ ($\sigma \in \Sigma$) from S into Θ instead of a "constant" (with respect to Σ) mapping N. This gives the so-called *Mealy machine* [29] (or Mealy automaton) which can be defined as the quintuple $\hat{A} = (S, \Sigma, \Theta, M, N)$, where S, Σ, M are as before, Θ is a finite set of outputs, and

$$N = \{N_\sigma\} \qquad (\sigma \in \Sigma)$$

is a set of mappings from S into Θ.

If, for every $\sigma \in \Sigma$,

$$pr_1 M_\sigma = S \quad \text{and} \quad pr_1 N_\sigma = S$$

95

(i.e., all M_σ and N_σ are mappings "of" S), the corresponding automaton is said to be a *complete* one, otherwise it is *incomplete*.

It can be shown that all the above-mentioned types of automata are in a certain sense equivalent. Here Mealy machines will be considered. Let

$$x = \sigma_1 \sigma_2 \ldots \sigma_k \ (\sigma_i \in \Sigma) \text{ be a word in } \Sigma^*.$$

The relations

$$N_{\sigma_1}, M_{\sigma_1} N_{\sigma_2}, \ldots, M_{\sigma_1} M_{\sigma_2} \ldots M_{\sigma_{k-1}} N_{\sigma_k} = M_{\sigma_1 \cdots \sigma_{k-1}} N_{\sigma_k} \quad (1)$$

describe the outputs of $\hat{A}$ when x is applied to the automaton. The actual output word depends on the state in which $\hat{A}$ is at the start of the experiment. If $\hat{A}$ is in state s and the word $x = \sigma_1 \ldots \sigma_k$ is applied, the consecutive outputs will be:

$$sN_{\sigma_1}, sM_{\sigma_1} N_{\sigma_2}, \ldots, sM_{\sigma_1 \cdots \sigma_{k-1}} N_{\sigma_k}.$$

Expressions (1) describe the output words for all starting points, and this is one of the advantages of the relational description of the automaton.

$$N_x = M_{\sigma_1} M_{\sigma_2} \ldots M_{\sigma_{k-1}} N_{\sigma_k} = M_{\sigma_1 \sigma_2 \cdots \sigma_{k-1}} N_{\sigma_k}$$

describes the "last output" when x is applied.

Notice that if $\hat{A}$ is not complete, some of the relations in (1) may be empty.

5.2   Coverings of Automata

An automaton $\hat{A} = (S, \Sigma, \Theta, M, N)$ can be regarded as a translator from Σ^* into Θ^*. Actually, it is a set of translators, because the output word in Θ^* depends not only on the input word from Σ^*, but also on the state $s \in S$ in which $\hat{A}$ is started.

It is natural to look for a simpler machine than the given $\hat{A}$, but one still capable of performing all tasks done by $\hat{A}$.

The notion "simpler" is, of course, relative. Simplicity of an automaton can be measured, e.g., by the number of its states. A device consisting of a number of smaller automata or, in some sense, standard automata interconnected in certain ways may also be considered as simpler than $\hat{A}$.

The meaning of "being capable of performing the tasks done by $\hat{A}$" will be made precise by the following definition [12]:

DEFINITION.   The automaton

$$\hat{B} = (S^B, \Sigma, \Theta, M^B, N^B)$$

is said to cover the automaton

$$\hat{A} = (S^A, \Sigma, \Theta, M^A, N^A),$$

notation $\hat{B} \geq \hat{A}$, if there exists a mapping χ of S^A into S^B, such that for every word $x \in \Sigma^*$

$$N_x^A \subseteq \chi N_x^B. \tag{2}$$

As can be seen from the notation, it is assumed that both automata have the same inputs and outputs. This limitation can be easily removed by introducing mappings from the input set of one automaton into that of the other and the same for the output sets, if these sets are different. Later such a mapping will be used, but at this stage the above assumption makes things more convenient, without invalidating the generality of the discussion.

The meaning of (2) is that to every state s^A in S^A there corresponds at least one state $s^B \in S^B$, such that when started in s^B, $\hat{B}$ performs all translations done by $\hat{A}$ started in s^A.

The relation of covering is easily seen to be reflexive and transitive, but not symmetric. If for some $\hat{A}$ and $\hat{B}$, $\hat{B} \geq \hat{A}$ and $\hat{A} \geq \hat{B}$, these automata are said to be *equivalent*.

If $\hat{A}$ is complete, N_x^A is a mapping of S^A into Θ; so is χN_x^B, and (2) becomes an equality. Nevertheless, even in this case $\hat{A}$ and $\hat{B}$ need not be equivalent; there can be states in S^B which do not correspond by χ to any state in S^A, and thus it is possible that $\hat{B}$ can perform translations of which $\hat{A}$ is not capable.

If for every two states s_1^A, $s_2^A \in S^A$, there exists at least one $x \in \Sigma^*$ such that

$$\phi \neq s_1^A N_x^A \neq s_2^A N_x^A \neq \phi,$$

the automaton $\hat{A}$ is called *reduced*. There are known constructions of reduced automata which cover a given automaton $\hat{A}$; moreover, in the complete case such a reduced automaton is unique up to renaming of its states (cf. 3.4).

5.3   Homomorphisms of Automata

DEFINITION.   Given the automata $\hat{A}$ and $\hat{B}$, the mapping ζ of S^A onto S^B is a *homomorphism* of $\hat{A}$ onto $\hat{B}$ if for every $\sigma \in \Sigma$:

(i) $M_\sigma^A \zeta \subseteq \zeta M_\sigma^B$

(ii) $N_\sigma^A \subseteq \zeta N_\sigma^B.$ (3)

For $\hat{A}$ and $\hat{B}$ complete one obtains in (3):

$$\text{(i)}\quad M_\sigma^A \zeta = \zeta M_\sigma^B,$$

which means that the semiautomaton B is a homomorphic image of A (cf. 2.4);

$$\text{(ii)}\quad N_\sigma^A = \zeta N_\sigma^B,$$

which is, in case of a recognizer, the requirement appearing in the definition of homomorphism in Section 3.4 (final states of $\hat{A}$, and only they are mapped onto final states of $\hat{B}$).

DEFINITION.   Given the automata $\hat{A}$ and $\hat{B}$ and a binary relation ψ

with $pr_1\psi = S^A$ and $pr_2\psi = S^B$, the relation ψ is a *weak homomorphism* of $\hat{A}$ onto $\hat{B}$ if, for every $\sigma \in \Sigma$:

(i) $\psi^{-1}M_\sigma^A \subseteq M_\sigma^B\psi^{-1}$

(ii) $\psi^{-1}N_\sigma^A \subseteq N_\sigma^B.$

$$(4)$$

Notice that if ψ is a mapping of S^A onto S^B, conditions (3) and (4) are equivalent, i.e., every homomorphism is also a weak homomorphism, and a weak homomorphism in which ψ is a mapping is a homomorphism. Indeed, if ψ is a mapping of S^A onto S^B, then $\psi\psi^{-1} \supseteq I_{S^A}$ (the identity on S^A) and $\psi^{-1}\psi = I_{S^B}$.
It follows:

$$M_\sigma^A\psi \subseteq \psi M_\sigma^B \Rightarrow \psi^{-1}M_\sigma^A\psi\psi^{-1} \subseteq \psi^{-1}\psi M_\sigma^B\psi^{-1} \Rightarrow \psi^{-1}M_\sigma^A \subseteq M_\sigma^B\psi^{-1}$$

$$N_\sigma^A \subseteq \psi N_\sigma^B \Rightarrow \psi^{-1}N_\sigma^A \subseteq \psi^{-1}\psi N_\sigma^B = N_\sigma^B$$

i.e., (3) $\Rightarrow$ (4). Conversely, with such a ψ

$$\psi^{-1}M_\sigma^A \subseteq M_\sigma^B\psi^{-1} \Rightarrow \psi\psi^{-1}M_\sigma^A\psi \subseteq \psi M_\sigma^B\psi^{-1}\psi \Rightarrow M_\sigma^A\psi \subseteq \psi M_\sigma^B$$

$$\psi^{-1}N_\sigma^A \subseteq N_\sigma^B \Rightarrow \psi\psi^{-1}N_\sigma^A \subseteq \psi N_\sigma^B \Rightarrow N_\sigma^A \subseteq \psi N_\sigma^B$$

i.e., (4) $\Rightarrow$ (3).
It is easy to construct examples of relations ψ for which conditions (3) and (4) are not equivalent.

5.4 Homomorphism and Covering

The advantage in using weak homomorphism is that it is often possible to find a relation satisfying (4), while there is no mapping doing this, and, nevertheless, the following is true:

THEOREM.   Let ψ be a weak homomorphism of $\hat{A}$ onto $\hat{B}$. Then $\hat{B} \geq \hat{A}$.

Proof.   (4) implies for any word $x = \sigma_1 \ldots \sigma_k$:

$$\psi^{-1} M_x^A = \psi^{-1} M_{\sigma_1}^A \ldots M_{\sigma_k}^A$$

$$\subseteq M_{\sigma_1}^B \psi^{-1} M_{\sigma_2}^A \ldots M_{\sigma_k}^A \subseteq M_{\sigma_1}^B M_{\sigma_2}^B \ldots M_{\sigma_k}^B \psi^{-1} = M_x^B \psi^{-1}$$

and

$$\psi^{-1} N_x^A = \psi^{-1} M_{\sigma_1}^A \ldots M_{\sigma_{k-1}}^A N_{\sigma_k}^A$$

$$\subseteq M_{\sigma_1}^B \ldots M_{\sigma_{k-1}}^B \psi^{-1} N_{\sigma_k}^A \subseteq M_{\sigma_1}^B \ldots M_{\sigma_{k-1}}^B N_{\sigma_k}^B = N_x^B.$$

$pr_1\psi = S^A$, $pr_2\psi = S^B$, and, clearly, it is always possible to find a mapping χ of S^A into S^B such that $\chi \subseteq \psi$. For any $x \in \Sigma^*$:

$$\psi^{-1} N_x^A \subseteq N_x^B \Rightarrow \chi^{-1} N_x^A \subseteq N_x^B \Rightarrow \chi\chi^{-1} N_x^A \subseteq \chi N_x^B.$$

But $pr_1\chi = S^A$, hence, $\chi\chi^{-1} \supseteq I_{S^A}$, and one obtains:

$$N_x^A \subseteq \chi N_x^B$$

i.e., $\hat{B} \geq \hat{A}$.

Of course, $\hat{B} \geq \hat{A}$ does not imply that $\hat{B}$ is a homomorphic or even a weak homomorphic image of $\hat{A}$.

5.5   Admissible Output-Consistent Decompositions

The notion of weak homomorphism leads to the following additional concepts. Let ψ be a weak homomorphism of $\hat{A}$ onto $\hat{B}$ and consider the following subsets of S^A:

$$\pi = \{H_i = s_i\psi^{-1}\}_{s_i \in S^B}.$$

$pr_1\psi = S^A$, hence, every element of S^A belongs to at least one subset of π. A collection of subsets of S^A having the last property is called a *decomposition* of S^A and the H_i's are called *blocks* of the decomposition. There may be blocks included in other blocks and even equal (but distinctly labelled) blocks in a decomposition. In the special case, when $H_i \cap H_j = \phi$, $i \neq j$ (i.e., the blocks of π are disjoint), the decomposition turns out to be a partition of S^A. Now,

$$H_i M_\sigma^A = s_i \psi^{-1} M_\sigma^A \subseteq s_i M_\sigma^B \psi^{-1} = s_j \psi^{-1} = H_j;$$

i.e., for every $\sigma \in \Sigma$ and every block H_i of the above π, there exists in π at least one block H_j including the set $H_i M_\sigma^A$. Such a decomposition is called an *admissible decomposition* of S^A.

Next, compute

$$H_i N_x^A = s_i \psi^{-1} N_x^A \subseteq s_i N_x^B.$$

The result shows that all elements in a block of π give the same output (if at all), when the same input word is applied to them—π is said to be an *output-consistent decomposition*.

Hence, the following theorem:

THEOREM.   A weak homomorphism ψ of $\hat{A}$ onto $\hat{B}$ induces naturally an admissible, output-consistent decomposition π of S^A: the blocks of π are the subsets of elements of S^A which are in the relation ψ with the same element of S^B.

Conversely, an admissible and output-consistent decomposition π of S^A leads naturally to at least one so-called π-*factor* of $\hat{A}$ (notation $\hat{A}/\pi$). This is an automaton $\hat{B}$ constructed in the following way: First,

$$\Sigma^B = \Sigma^A \quad \text{and} \quad \Theta^B = \Theta^A.$$

The states of $\hat{B}$ will be the blocks of π. As in Section 1.11, a block H_i of π, i.e., a subset of S^A when considered as an element of S^B, will be denoted by $\overline{H}_i$.

For every $\sigma \in \Sigma$ and every H_i there exists at least one H_j such that $H_i M_\sigma^A \subseteq H_j$. Take arbitrarily one of such H_j's and define

$$\overline{H}_i M_\sigma^B = \overline{H}_j.$$

N^B is defined by

$$\bar{H}_i N_\sigma^B = H_i N_\sigma^A,$$

and the output-consistency of π ensures that the right-hand side consists of one element of Θ, or it is empty.

For every such π-factor $\hat{B}$ of $\hat{A}$, the relation ψ with $pr_1\psi = S^A$ and $pr_2\psi = S^B$ given by:

$$\left(\frac{s^A}{\bar{H}_i}\right) \in \psi \Leftrightarrow s^A \in H_i \qquad (s^A \in S^A)$$

is a weak homomorphism of $\hat{A}$ onto $\hat{B}$. Indeed, for every $\bar{H}_i \in S^B$ and every $\sigma \in \Sigma$

$$\bar{H}_i\psi^{-1}M_\sigma^A = H_i M_\sigma^A \subseteq H_j = \bar{H}_j\psi^{-1} = \bar{H}_i M_\sigma^B\psi^{-1}$$

and

$$\bar{H}_i\psi^{-1}N_\sigma^A = H_i N_\sigma^A = \bar{H}_i N_\sigma^B;$$

i.e., conditions (4) are satisfied.

Altogether one has the following theorem:

THEOREM.   An admissible output-consistent decomposition π of S^A determines at least one automaton (a π-factor of $\hat{A}$) which is a weakly homomorphic image of $\hat{A}$.

In the special case, when π is an admissible output-consistent partition of S^A, $\hat{A}/\pi$ is unique. The above relation ψ becomes in this case a mapping, consequently, a homomorphism of $\hat{A}$ onto $\hat{A}/\pi$ (cf. 3.5).

EXAMPLE.

$$\hat{A} = \{\{1, 2, 3, 4, 5, 6, 7, 8\}, \{0, 1\}, \{0, 1\}, M^A, N^A\},$$

where

$$M_\sigma^A = \begin{pmatrix} 1 & 2 & 3 & 4 & 6 & 7 & 8 \\ 6 & 8 & 5 & 3 & 4 & 6 & 7 \end{pmatrix}, \qquad M_1^A = \begin{pmatrix} 2 & 3 & 4 & 5 & 6 & 7 & 8 \\ 2 & 2 & 7 & 2 & 1 & 5 & 3 \end{pmatrix}$$

$$N_0^A = \begin{pmatrix} 1 & 4 & 5 & 6 & 8 \\ 0 & 1 & 1 & 1 & 1 \end{pmatrix}, \qquad N_1^A = \begin{pmatrix} 1 & 3 & 4 & 6 & 7 & 8 \\ 0 & 0 & 1 & 0 & 1 & 0 \end{pmatrix}.$$

$$\pi = \{H_1 = \{1, 2, 3\}, \qquad H_2 = \{3, 5, 6, 8\}, \qquad H_3 = \{2, 4, 5, 7\}\}$$

is an admissible output-consistent decomposition of S. Indeed:

$$H_1 M_0^A = \{5, 6, 8\} \subseteq H_2 \qquad H_1 M_1^A = \{2\} \subseteq H_1 \quad \text{and} \quad H_3$$
$$H_2 M_0^A = \{4, 5, 7\} \subseteq H_3 \qquad H_2 M_1^A = \{1, 2, 3\} = H_1$$
$$H_3 M_0^A = \{3, 6, 8\} \subseteq H_2 \qquad H_3 M_1^A = \{2, 5, 7\} \subseteq H_3.$$

Hence, π is admissible. Now,

$$H_1 N_0^A = \{0\}, \qquad H_1 N_1^A = \{0\}, \qquad H_2 N_0^A = \{1\},$$
$$H_2 N_1^A = \{0\}, \qquad H_3 N_0^A = \{1\}, \qquad H_3 N_1^A = \{1\};$$

i.e., π is output-consistent.

Let $\hat{B}$ be the following π-factor of $\hat{A}$:

$$\hat{B} = \{\{\overline{H}_1, \overline{H}_2, \overline{H}_3\}, \{0, 1\}, \{0, 1\}, M^B, N^B\},$$

where

$$M_0^B = \begin{pmatrix} \overline{H}_1 & \overline{H}_2 & \overline{H}_3 \\ \overline{H}_2 & \overline{H}_3 & \overline{H}_2 \end{pmatrix} \qquad M_1^B = \begin{pmatrix} \overline{H}_1 & \overline{H}_2 & \overline{H}_3 \\ \overline{H}_1 & \overline{H}_1 & \overline{H}_3 \end{pmatrix}$$

$$N_0^B = \begin{pmatrix} \overline{H}_1 & \overline{H}_2 & \overline{H}_3 \\ 0 & 1 & 1 \end{pmatrix} \qquad N_1^B = \begin{pmatrix} \overline{H}_1 & \overline{H}_2 & \overline{H}_3 \\ 0 & 0 & 1 \end{pmatrix}.$$

$\overline{H}_1 M_1^B$ could be also defined as $\overline{H}_3$, leading to a distinct π-factor of $\hat{A}$. Notice also that $\hat{B}$ is complete although $\hat{A}$ is not. This is clearly not necessary, i.e., $\hat{B}$ can be incomplete together with $\hat{A}$. (Of course, if $\hat{A}$ is complete, so is $\hat{B}$.)

$\hat{B}$ is a weak homomorphic image of $\hat{A}$. Indeed, consider the relation:

$$\psi = \begin{pmatrix} 1 & 2 & 2 & 3 & 3 & 4 & 5 & 5 & 6 & 7 & 8 \\ \overline{H}_1 & \overline{H}_1 & \overline{H}_3 & \overline{H}_1 & \overline{H}_2 & \overline{H}_3 & \overline{H}_2 & \overline{H}_3 & \overline{H}_2 & \overline{H}_3 & \overline{H}_2 \end{pmatrix}$$

$$\psi^{-1}M_0^A = \begin{pmatrix} \overline{H}_1 & \overline{H}_1 & \overline{H}_1 & \overline{H}_2 & \overline{H}_2 & \overline{H}_2 & \overline{H}_3 & \overline{H}_3 & \overline{H}_3 \\ 5 & 6 & 8 & 4 & 5 & 7 & 3 & 6 & 8 \end{pmatrix}$$

$$M_0^B\psi^{-1} = \begin{pmatrix} \overline{H}_1 & \overline{H}_1 & \overline{H}_1 & \overline{H}_1 & \overline{H}_2 & \overline{H}_2 & \overline{H}_2 & \overline{H}_2 & \overline{H}_3 & \overline{H}_3 & \overline{H}_3 & \overline{H}_3 \\ 3 & 5 & 6 & 8 & 2 & 4 & 5 & 7 & 3 & 5 & 6 & 8 \end{pmatrix}$$

$$\psi^{-1}M_0^A \subseteq M_0^B\psi^{-1}$$

$$\psi^{-1}M_1^A = \begin{pmatrix} \overline{H}_1 & \overline{H}_2 & \overline{H}_2 & \overline{H}_2 & \overline{H}_3 & \overline{H}_3 & \overline{H}_3 \\ 2 & 1 & 2 & 3 & 2 & 5 & 7 \end{pmatrix}$$

$$M_1^B\psi^{-1} = \begin{pmatrix} \overline{H}_1 & \overline{H}_1 & \overline{H}_1 & \overline{H}_2 & \overline{H}_2 & \overline{H}_2 & \overline{H}_3 & \overline{H}_3 & \overline{H}_3 & \overline{H}_3 \\ 1 & 2 & 3 & 1 & 2 & 3 & 2 & 4 & 5 & 7 \end{pmatrix}$$

$$\psi^{-1}M_1^A \subseteq M_1^B\psi^{-1}$$

$$\psi^{-1}N_0^A = \begin{pmatrix} \overline{H}_1 & \overline{H}_2 & \overline{H}_3 \\ 0 & 1 & 1 \end{pmatrix} \subseteq N_0^B, \qquad \psi^{-1}N_1^A = \begin{pmatrix} \overline{H}_1 & \overline{H}_2 & \overline{H}_3 \\ 0 & 0 & 1 \end{pmatrix} \subseteq N_1^B.$$

It follows from the theorem in Section 5.4 that $\hat{B} \geq \hat{A}$. To illustrate this notion assume that $\hat{A}$ is in state 5 and the input $x = 1001$ is applied to it. The last output is

$$\{5\}M_1^A M_0^A M_0^A N_1^A = 1.$$

The state 5 in $\hat{A}$ can be covered either by $\overline{H}_2$ or by $\overline{H}_3$ in $\hat{B}$. Assume that in χ of (2) one puts $\left(\dfrac{5}{\overline{H}_2}\right)$. Then:

$$\{5\}\chi N_x^B = \overline{H}_2 M_1^B M_0^B M_0^B N_1^B = 1,$$

the same output as before.

5.6   Reduction of Covering of an Automaton
to Covering of a Semiautomaton

The problem of finding an automaton $\hat{B}$, having some desired properties and covering a given $\hat{A}$, is often convenient to solve in two steps:
(a) to construct an appropriate semiautomaton B; (b) to supply B with
outputs so that the obtained $\hat{B}$ will cover $\hat{A}$.

To this end covering of semiautomata will be defined.

DEFINITION.   The semiautomaton $B = (S^B, \Sigma, M^B)$ covers the semiautomaton $A = (S^A, \Sigma, M^A)$, $B \geq A$, if there exists a mapping η of a
subset of S^B onto S^A such that for every $\sigma \in \Sigma$:

$$\eta M_\sigma^A \subseteq M_\sigma^B \eta. \tag{5}$$

Notice that no one of the two relations $B \geq A$ and $\hat{B} \geq \hat{A}$ (where B
and A are the semiautomata of $\hat{B}$ and $\hat{A}$, respectively) implies the other.

Nevertheless, the two-step construction mentioned above is possible
because of the following theorem:

THEOREM.   Let $\hat{A}$ be an automaton and B a semiautomaton covering
the semiautomaton A of $\hat{A}$. Then there exists an automaton $\hat{B}$ with B as
its semiautomaton such that $\hat{B} \geq \hat{A}$.

Proof.   By assumption there exists a mapping η of a subset of S^B
*onto S^A, satisfying (5). Define

$$N_\sigma^B = \eta N_\sigma^A \qquad (\sigma \in \Sigma).$$

In general, this defines the N_σ^B's only on subsets of S^B; for the remaining
elements of S^B they can be chosen arbitrarily. There exists, obviously,
a mapping χ of S^A into S^B such that $\chi \subseteq \eta^{-1}$ (notice that $pr_2\eta =
pr_1\eta^{-1} = S^A$). For any $x = \sigma_1 \ldots \sigma_k \in \Sigma^*$:

$$\chi^{-1}N_x^A \subseteq \eta N_x^A = \eta M_{\sigma_1}^A \ldots M_{\sigma_{k-1}}^A N_{\sigma_k}^A \subseteq M_{\sigma_1}^B \ldots M_{\sigma_{k-1}}^B \eta N_{\sigma_k}^A$$
$$\subseteq M_{\sigma_1}^B \ldots M_{\sigma_{k-1}}^B N_{\sigma_k}^B = N_x^B.$$

Hence

$$N_x^A \subseteq \chi\chi^{-1}N_x^A \subseteq \chi N_x^B,$$

and the obtained automaton $\hat{B}$ (having the given B as its semiautomaton) covers the automaton $\hat{A}$.

For a reduced automaton $\hat{A}$ the following is also true:

$$\hat{B} \geq \hat{A} \Rightarrow B \geq A.$$

Indeed, $\hat{B} \geq \hat{A} \Rightarrow \exists$ a mapping χ of S^A into S^B such that for every $x \in \Sigma^*$, $N_x^A \subseteq \chi N_x^B$, i.e., for every $s^A \in S^A$

$$s^A N_x^A \neq \phi \Rightarrow s^A N_x^A = s^A \chi N_x^B.$$

Hence, $s_1^A \chi = s_2^A \chi \Rightarrow s_1^A N_x^A = s_2^A N_x^A$ for every $x \in \Sigma^*$ for which both expressions exist, and, as $\hat{A}$ is reduced, this implies $s_1^A = s_2^A$.

Thus, χ is one-to-one and χ^{-1} is a mapping of a subset of S^B onto S^A.

To prove that $B \geq A$ one must find a mapping η from a subset of S^B onto S^A satisfying (5).

In general, χ^{-1} cannot serve as η, because there may be states $s^B \in S^B$ and inputs $\sigma \in \Sigma$ such that $s^B \chi^{-1} \neq \phi$, but $s^B M_\sigma^B \chi^{-1} = \phi$.†

Consider, for example, the following (complete) automata:

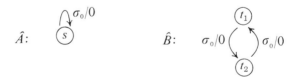

$$\hat{A}: \qquad \hat{B}:$$

(Explanation of the notation: if $s_i M_{\sigma_k} = s_j$ and $s_i N_{\sigma_k} = \theta$, an arrow marked by σ_k/θ leads from s_i to s_j.) $\hat{A}$ is reduced and $\hat{B} \geq \hat{A}$, because for $\chi = \begin{pmatrix} s \\ t_1 \end{pmatrix}$ one obtains $N_x^A = \chi N_x^B$ for any $x \in \Sigma^*$.

---

† This remark, the definition of η and the subsequent proof belong to Professor Albert R. Meyer.

Now, $\chi^{-1} = \begin{pmatrix} t_1 \\ s \end{pmatrix}$ and $t_1 \chi^{-1} M_{\sigma_0}^A = s M_{\sigma_0}^A = s$, but $t_1 M_{\sigma_0}^B \chi^{-1} = t_2 \chi^{-1} = \phi$, i.e., $\chi^{-1} M_{\sigma_0}^A \nsubseteq M_{\sigma_0}^B \chi^{-1}$.

One looks for a mapping η such that for any $x \in \Sigma^*$ and any $s^A \in S^A$

$$s^A \chi M_x^B \eta = s^A M_x^A,$$

provided that both sides $\neq \phi$.

Accordingly, put

$$\eta = \bigcup_{x \in \Sigma^*} (\chi M_x^B)^{-1} M_x^A.$$

$\mathrm{pr}_2\, \eta \subseteq S^A$, but $\eta \supseteq \chi^{-1}$, hence $\mathrm{pr}_2\, \eta \supseteq \mathrm{pr}_2\, \chi^{-1} = S^A$, i.e., $\mathrm{pr}_2\, \eta = S^A$.

The next assertion is that η is a mapping (of a subset of S^B onto S^A).

χM_x^B is a mapping, hence $(\chi M_x^B)^{-1} \chi M_x^B \subseteq I_{S^B}$.

For any $y \in \Sigma^* - \{\wedge\}$

$$\eta N_y^A = \bigcup_{x \in \Sigma^*} (\chi M_x^B)^{-1} M_x^A N_y^A = \bigcup_{x \in \Sigma^*} (\chi M_x^B)^{-1} N_{xy}^A \subseteq \bigcup_{x \in \Sigma^*} (\chi M_x^B)^{-1} \chi N_{xy}^B$$

$$= \bigcup_{x \in \Sigma^*} (\chi M_x^B)^{-1} \chi M_x^B N_y^B \subseteq N_y^B.$$

If now, $s_1^A, s_2^A \in s^B \eta$, then for every $y \in \Sigma^*$ for which $s_1^A N_y^A \neq \phi \neq s_2^A N_y^A$ one obtains $s_1^A N_y^A, s_2^A N_y^A \in s^B \eta N_y^A \subseteq s^B N_y^B$, and since $s^B N_y^B \neq \phi$ is a singleton $s_1^A N_y^A = s_2^A N_y^A$. But $\hat{A}$ is reduced and consequently $s_1^A = s_2^A$ i.e., η is really a mapping.

It follows that η can be computed using only those (shortest) $x \in \Sigma^*$ for which $(\chi M_x^B)^{-1} M_x^A \neq \phi$ and which lead from states of $S^A \chi$ to all states of S^B accessible from $S^A \chi$.

The mapping η satisfies (5). To prove this notice first that

$$s^B \eta M_\sigma^A \neq \phi \Rightarrow \exists\, y \in \Sigma^*$$

such that $s^B \eta M_\sigma^A N_y^A \neq \phi$, because output-empty states do not appear in a reduced automaton.

Next,

$$s^B \eta M_\sigma^A N_y^A = s^B \eta N_{\sigma y}^A = s^B N_{\sigma y}^B = s^B M_\sigma^B N_y^B,$$

consequently $s^B M_\sigma^B \neq \phi$, i.e., $s^B \in \mathrm{pr}_1 \, M_\sigma^B$ and $\begin{pmatrix} s^B \\ s^B \end{pmatrix} \in M_\sigma^B (M_\sigma^B)^{-1}$.

Altogether, for any s^B and σ such that $s^B \eta M_\sigma^A \neq \phi$

$$s^B \eta M_\sigma^A = s^B (\bigcup_{x \in \Sigma^*} (\chi M_x^B)^{-1} M_x^A) M_\sigma^A \subseteq s^B M_\sigma^B (M_\sigma^B)^{-1} (\bigcup_{x \in \Sigma^*} (\chi M_x^B)^{-1} M_x^A) M_\sigma^A$$

$$= s^B M_\sigma^B (\bigcup_{x \in \Sigma^*} (\chi M_{x\sigma}^B)^{-1} M_{x\sigma}^A) \subseteq s^B M_\sigma^B \eta.$$

Thus, $\eta M_\sigma^A \subseteq M_\sigma^B \eta$.

Since for every automaton there exists at least one reduced automaton covering it, the problem of finding covers of automata can always be reduced (having in mind the theorem of this section) to looking for covers of semiautomata. This will be done in what follows.

5.7   Properties of Coverings of Semiautomata

In the following it will always be assumed (without mentioning this explicitly) that *the semiautomata considered are complete*, and the mapping M_x^A of S^A into S^A will be denoted by x^A ($x \in \Sigma^*$). N_x^A will not appear because the discussion is limited to semiautomata only.

In this section some properties of the notion of covering of semi-automata are derived. First, the definition of covering will be extended to the case when $\Sigma^A \neq \Sigma^B$:

DEFINITION.   The semiautomaton $B = (S^B, \Sigma^B, M^B)$ covers the semiautomaton $A = (S^A, \Sigma^A, M^A)$ if there exist a mapping η of a subset of S^B onto S^A, and a mapping ξ of Σ^A into Σ^B, such that for every $\sigma \in \Sigma^A$:

$$\eta \sigma^A \subseteq (\sigma \xi)^B \eta \tag{6}$$

(i.e., to every input in A there corresponds an input in B "doing at least the same").

Notice that if $B \geq A$, then

$$\sigma_1^A \neq \sigma_2^A \Rightarrow (\sigma_1 \xi)^B \neq (\sigma_2 \xi)^B.$$

Indeed, assume that for some $s^A \in S^A$, $s^A \sigma_1^A \neq s^A \sigma_2^A$. Take an $s^B \in S^B$ such that $s^B \eta = s^A$ (η is a mapping *onto* S^A; hence, such an s^B must exist). Then

$$s^B \eta \sigma_1^A = s^A \sigma_1^A \neq s^A \sigma_2^A = s^B \eta \sigma_2^A.$$

If now $(\sigma_1 \xi)^B = (\sigma_2 \xi)^B$, then $s^B(\sigma_1 \xi)^B \eta = s^B(\sigma_2 \xi)^B \eta$ and (6) cannot hold simultaneously for σ_1 and σ_2 (the expressions at both sides of (6) are mappings).

In words, ξ can coincide equal inputs of A only, and if all inputs in A are distinct, ξ must be one-to-one. Thus, the introduction of ξ in the definition of covering is not essential—one would rather coincide the equal inputs of the covered semiautomaton and use the definition from Section 5.6. This will be done in the sequel often.

Notice, accordingly, the following simple cases of covering:

(a)   The semiautomaton B obtained from A by coinciding equal inputs in A covers A and is covered by A. One has also, clearly, $G_B = G_A$.

(b)   Given an A, one can add new inputs to Σ^A. The obtained semiautomaton will cover A.

LEMMA A.   If ξ is one-to-one, then $B \geq A \Leftrightarrow A$ is a homomorphic image of a subsemiautomaton of B.

Proof. $B \geq A \Rightarrow \exists$ a mapping η of a subset of S^B onto S^A and a mapping ξ (assumed here to be one-to-one) of Σ^A into Σ^B, such that $\eta \sigma^A \subseteq (\sigma \xi)^B \eta$ for every $\sigma \in \Sigma$.

The subset $S^{B'} = S^A \eta^{-1}$ forms a subsemiautomaton of B with respect to the inputs $\Sigma^A \xi$ of B:

$$s^B \in S^A \eta^{-1} \Rightarrow s^B \eta \sigma^A \neq \phi \Rightarrow s^B \eta \sigma^A = s^B(\sigma \xi)^B \eta \Rightarrow s^B(\sigma \xi)^B \in S^A \eta^{-1};$$

i.e., $S^{B'}$ is closed under the mappings in M^B corresponding to $\Sigma^A \xi$.

The last equality implies, also, that for the restriction $(\sigma\xi)^{B'}$ of $(\sigma\xi)^B$ to $S^{B'}$ one has

$$(\sigma\xi)^{B'}\eta = \eta\sigma^A \quad \text{or} \quad (\sigma\xi)^{B'}\eta = \eta[(\sigma\xi)\xi^{-1}]^A \tag{7}$$

($\xi\xi^{-1}$ is the identity on Σ^A).

Comparison with the definition in Section 2.4 shows that A is a homomorphic image of the subsemiautomaton B' of B, formed by the states $S^{B'} = S^A\eta^{-1}$ and the inputs $\Sigma^A\xi$.

Conversely, if A is a homomorphic image of a subsemiautomaton B' of B, there exist a mapping η of $S^{B'} \subseteq S^B$ onto S^A and a mapping ξ (assumed to be one-to-one) of $\Sigma^{B'} \subseteq \Sigma^B$ onto Σ^A, such that for every $\sigma \in \Sigma^A$:

$$(\sigma\xi^{-1})^{B'}\eta = \eta\sigma^A.$$

But $(\sigma\xi^{-1})^{B'} \subseteq (\sigma\xi^{-1})^B$, hence

$$\eta\sigma^A \subseteq (\sigma\xi^{-1})^B\eta$$

i.e., (6) is satisfied.

As mentioned, ξ is usually assumed to be the identity and then, of course, the lemma holds.

A simple corollary of the lemma is that if in the covering $B \geq A$ η is a one-to-one mapping of S^B onto S^A and ξ is a mapping of Σ^A onto Σ^B, then the semiautomaton obtained from A by coinciding the subsets of inputs having equal images under ξ is isomorphic to B.

LEMMA B. $B \geq A \Rightarrow G_A$ is a homomorphic image of a subsemigroup of G_B.

Proof.   Coinciding of equal inputs in Σ^A does not change G_A, hence one can assume that this is done. Then ξ is one-to-one, and by Lemma A, the semiautomaton A is a homomorphic image of a subsemiautomaton B' of B. By the theorem in Section 2.7, G_A is a homomorphic image of $G_{B'}$, and by the lemma in 2.4, $G_{B'}$ is a homomorphic image of a subsemigroup of G_B; thus, G_A is a homomorphic image of a subsemi-group of G_B.

Two additional facts will be mentioned:

(1) $B \geq A, C \geq B \Rightarrow C \geq A$ (apply the definition of covering)
(2) If π is an admissible *partition* of S^B and A is the π-factor of B, then $B \geq A$ (because A is a homomorphic image of B).

5.8 Construction of an Auxiliary Semiautomaton

In the sequel the following construction of M. Yoeli [44] will be useful. Given a semiautomaton $A = (S^A, \Sigma^A, M^A)$, an admissible de-composition π of S^A, and a π-factor $A/\pi = B$, a new semiautomaton $A^* = (S^{A^*}, \Sigma^{A^*}, M^{A^*})$ is constructed as follows:

$$\Sigma^{A^*} = \Sigma^A = \Sigma^B.$$

$S^{A^*} = \{(s^A, \overline{H}_i)\}, \qquad s^A \in S^A, \qquad \text{and} \qquad s^A \in H_i \in \pi.$

$(s^A, \overline{H}_i)\sigma^{A^*} = (s^A\sigma^A, \overline{H}_i\sigma^B) \qquad \text{for every} \quad \overline{\sigma \in \Sigma^A}.$
Notice that the obtained pair is necessarily an element of S^{A^*} because, by the construction of $A/\pi = B$,

$$s^A \in H_i \Rightarrow s^A\sigma^A \in H_j \qquad \text{where} \quad \overline{H}_j = \overline{H}_i\sigma^B.$$

The following two observations are important.

(i) Define a partition π^* of S^{A^*} such that the partition blocks con-sist of all pairs having the same second component. π^* is admissible because the mappings σ^{A^*} act independently on the components of s^{A^*}. A^*/π^* is isomorphic to $A/\pi = B$. Indeed, the blocks of π^* are in one-to-one correspondence with the elements of B, and the mappings in A^*/π^* originate from the mappings in B.

(ii)   The mapping η of S^{A^*} onto S^A defined by $(s^A, \bar{H}_i)\eta = s^A$ satisfies $\eta \sigma^A = \sigma^{A^*}\eta$ for every σ because

$$(s^A, \bar{H}_i)\eta \sigma^A = s^A \sigma^A$$

and

$$(s^A, \bar{H}_i)\sigma^{A^*}\eta = (s^A \sigma^A, \bar{H}_i \sigma^B)\eta = s^A \sigma^A \qquad \text{for all} \quad (s^A, \bar{H}_i) \in S^{A^*}.$$

Hence $A^* \geq A$.

Usually it is more convenient to work with partitions than with decompositions, and this is the reason for introducing A^*, which can be interpreted as the given A in which the states, belonging to more than one block of π, are appropriately "duplicated".

5.9   Direct Product of Semiautomata

Two semiautomata can be combined as in the following definition:

DEFINITION.   The *direct product* of the semiautomata $A = (S^A, \Sigma, M^A)$ and $B = (S^B, \Sigma, M^B)$ is the semiautomaton $A \times B = (S^{A \times B}, \Sigma, M^{A \times B})$ with $S^{A \times B} = S^A \times S^B$ and $M^{A \times B}$ defined as follows: For every $\sigma \in \Sigma$ and every $s^A \in S^A$, $s^B \in S^B$

$$(s^A, s^B)\sigma^{A \times B} = (s^A \sigma^A, s^B \sigma^B).$$

THEOREM.   Let π and τ be two admissible partitions of S^C in a semiautomaton C such that their intersection is the identity partition of S^C. Then $C/\pi \times C/\tau \geq C$.

Proof.   Let $A = C/\pi$, $B = C/\tau$.
Let $T^{A \times B} \subseteq S^{A \times B}$ be the set of all pairs

$$\{(\bar{H}_i, \bar{K}_j) \mid \bar{H}_i \in S^A, \bar{K}_j \in S^B, H_i \cap K_j \neq \phi\}.$$

The mapping η of $T^{A \times B}$ into S^C is defined by

$$(\bar{H}_i, \bar{K}_j)\eta = H_i \cap K_j.$$

It follows from $\pi\tau = \pi_{\text{iden}}$ of S^C that η is a one-to-one mapping of $T^{A \times B}$ *onto* S^C.

Let φ_π and φ_τ denote the natural mappings of S^C onto the blocks of π and τ, respectively; i.e., $s^C\varphi_\pi = H_i \Leftrightarrow s^C \in H_i$ and $s^C\varphi_\tau = K_j \Leftrightarrow s^C \in K_j$.

Now, for every $(\bar{H}_i, \bar{K}_j) \in T^{A \times B}$:

$$
\begin{aligned}
(\bar{H}_i, \bar{K}_j)\eta\sigma^C = (H_i \cap K_j)\sigma^C &= H_i\sigma^C \cap K_j\sigma^C \\
&= H_i\sigma^C\varphi_\pi \cap K_j\sigma^C\varphi_\tau \\
&= (\overline{H_i\sigma^C\varphi_\pi}, \overline{K_j\sigma^C\varphi_\tau})\eta \\
&= (\bar{H}_i\sigma^A, \bar{K}_j\sigma^B)\eta = (\bar{H}_i, \bar{K}_j)\sigma^{A \times B}\eta,
\end{aligned}
$$

and, consequently, $A \times B \geq C$.

The construction of a direct product can be, in an obvious way, generalized to any finite number of semiautomata with a common (or appropriately translated) set of inputs.

5.10 Cascade Product of Semiautomata

Two semiautomata can be connected as in the following definition:

DEFINITION. Let $A = (S^A, \Sigma^A, M^A)$ and $B = (S^B, \Sigma^B, M^B)$ be two semiautomata and ω a mapping of $S^A \times \Sigma^A$ into Σ^B. The *cascade product* of A and B with the mapping ω is the semiautomaton

$$A\overset{\circ}{\omega}B = (S^{A\overset{\circ}{\omega}B}, \Sigma^{A\overset{\circ}{\omega}B}, M^{A\overset{\circ}{\omega}B})$$

with

$$S^{A\overset{\circ}{\omega}B} = S^A \times S^B, \qquad \Sigma^{A\overset{\circ}{\omega}B} = \Sigma^A,$$

and $M^{A\mathring{\omega}B}$ defined by

$$(s^A, s^B)\sigma^{A\mathring{\omega}B} = (s^A\sigma_v^A, s^B((s^A, \sigma)\omega)^B), \qquad (s^A \in S^A, s^B \in S^B, \sigma \in \Sigma^A).$$

The case, when $S^A \times \Sigma^A \subseteq \Sigma^B$ and ω is the identity on $S^A \times \Sigma^A$, will be the usual one in what follows. The corresponding cascade product of A and B will be denoted by $A^\circ B$ and

$$(s^A, s^B)\sigma^{A^\circ B} = (s^A\sigma^A, s^B(s^A, \sigma)^B).$$

If $\Sigma^A = \Sigma^B$ and $(s^A, \sigma)\omega = \sigma$ for every s^A, then $A\mathring{\omega}B$ reduces to the direct product $A \times B$. Thus, the direct product can always be considered as a particular case of the cascade product.

The cascade product is associative, providing that the connecting mappings ω are properly interrelated.

Let $D = (A\mathring{\omega}_1 B)\mathring{\omega}_2 C$ and $F = A\mathring{\omega}_3(B\mathring{\omega}_4 C)$. Then

$$S^D = (A \times B) \times C = A \times B \times C = A \times (B \times C) = S^F$$
$$\Sigma^D = \Sigma^{A\mathring{\omega}_1 B} = \Sigma^A = \Sigma^F.$$

For any $s^A \in S^A$, $s^B \in S^B$, $s^C \in S^C$, and $\sigma \in \Sigma^A$:

$$(s^A, s^B, s^C)\sigma^D = ((s^A, s^B)\sigma^{A\mathring{\omega}_1 B}, s^C(((s^A, s^B), \sigma)\omega_2)^C)$$
$$= (s^A\sigma^A, s^B((s^A, \sigma)\omega_1)^B, s^C(((s^A, s^B), \sigma)\omega_2)^C),$$

and

$$(s^A, s^B, s^C)\sigma^F = (s^A\sigma^A, (s^B, s^C)((s^A, \sigma)\omega_3)^{B\mathring{\omega}_4 C})$$
$$= (s^A\sigma^A, s^B((s^A, \sigma)\omega_3)^B, s^C((s^B, (s^A, \sigma)\omega_3)\omega_4)^C).$$

Put $\omega_1 = \omega_3$ and choose $\omega_1, \omega_2, \omega_4$ so that

$$((s^A, s^B), \sigma)\omega_2 = (s^B, (s^A, \sigma)\omega_1)\omega_4$$

(for example, define ω_1 and ω_4, compute the right-hand side and define ω_2 accordingly). Then

$$(s^A, s^B, s^C)\sigma^D = (s^A, s^B, s^C)\sigma^F.$$

In case, when

$$S^A \times \Sigma^A \subseteq \Sigma^B, \qquad (S^A \times S^B) \times \Sigma^A \subseteq \Sigma^C, \qquad S^B \times \Sigma^B \subseteq \Sigma^C,$$

and

$$((s^A, s^B), \sigma)^C = (s^B, (s^A, \sigma))^C$$

(both inputs belong to Σ^C), one obtains

$$(A°B)°C = A°(B°C).$$

LEMMA A.   If $B \geq A$, then for every $C\mathring{\omega}_2 A$ there exists an ω_1 such that $C\mathring{\omega}_1 B \geq C\mathring{\omega}_2 A$.

Proof. $B \geq A \Rightarrow$ (6) in Section 5.7 holds.
Define a mapping η' of $S^C \times S^A \eta^{-1}$ onto $S^C \times S^A$ by

$$(s^C, s^B)\eta' = (s^C, s^B\eta)$$

for any $s^C \in S^C$ and any $s^B \in S^A \eta^{-1}$.
For every $s^C \in S^C$ and $\sigma \in \Sigma^C$ define:

$$(s^C, \sigma)\omega_1 = (s^C, \sigma)\omega_2\xi.$$

Then, for every $(s^C, s^B) \subset S^C \times S^A \eta^{-1} \subseteq S^{C\mathring{\omega}_1 B}$ and every $\sigma \in \Sigma^C$:

$$
\begin{aligned}
(s^C, s^B)\eta'\sigma^{C\mathring{\omega}_2 A} &= (s^C, s^B\eta)\sigma^{C\mathring{\omega}_2 A} \\
&= (s^C\sigma^C, s^B\eta((s^C, \sigma)\omega_2)^A) \qquad \text{[by (6)]} \\
&= (s^C\sigma^C, s^B((s^C, \sigma)\omega_2\xi)^B\eta) \\
&= (s^C\sigma^C, s^B((s^C, \sigma)\omega_1)^B\eta) \\
&= (s^C\sigma^C, s^B((s^C, \sigma)\omega_1)^B)\eta' \\
&= (s^C, s^B)\sigma^{C\mathring{\omega}_1 B}\eta',
\end{aligned}
$$

and so

$$C \overset{\circ}{\omega}_1 B \geq C \overset{\circ}{\omega}_2 A$$

(notice that both automata have the same inputs).

In the important special case, when $C^\circ A$ is defined and $B \geq A$ with ξ an identity, $C^\circ B$ is also defined, and $C^\circ B \geq C^\circ A$.

"Multiplying from right" requires some additional precautions.

LEMMA B.   If $B \geq A$ with ξ a one-to-one mapping, then for every $A \overset{\circ}{\omega}_2 C$ there exists an ω_1 such that $B \overset{\circ}{\omega}_1 C \geq A \overset{\circ}{\omega}_2 C$.

Proof. $B \geq A \Rightarrow$ (6) in Section 5.7 holds. Define a mapping η' of $S^A \eta^{-1} \times S^C$ onto $S^A \times S^C = S^{A \overset{\circ}{\omega}_2 C}$ such that for any $s^B \in S^A \eta^{-1}$ and any $s^C \in S^C$:

$$(s^B, s^C)\eta' = (s^B \eta, s^C).$$

Define a mapping ω_1 of $S^B \times \Sigma^B$ into Σ^C in the following way: if $s^B \in S^A \eta^{-1}$ and $\sigma \in \Sigma^A$, then $(s^B, \sigma\xi)\omega_1 = (s^B \eta, \sigma)\omega_2$, (here the fact that ξ is one-to-one is used); for other pairs $(s^B, $ input of $B)$ the image under ω_1 is defined arbitrarily.

Now, for any $(s^B, s^C) \in S^A \eta^{-1} \times S^C \subseteq S^{B \overset{\circ}{\omega}_1 C}$ and any $\sigma \in \Sigma^A$:

$$(s^B, s^C)\eta' \sigma^{A \overset{\circ}{\omega}_2 C} = (s^B \eta, s^C)\sigma^{A \overset{\circ}{\omega}_2 C}$$

$$= (s^B \eta \sigma^A, s^C((s^B \eta, \sigma)\omega_2)^C) \qquad \text{(by (6) and definition of } \omega_1\text{)}$$

$$= (s^B (\sigma\xi)^B \eta, s^C((s^B, \sigma\xi)\omega_1)^C)$$

$$= (s^B (\sigma\xi)^B, s^C((s^B, \sigma\xi)\omega_1)^C)\eta'$$

$$= (s^B, s^C)(\sigma\xi)^{B \overset{\circ}{\omega}_1 C}\eta'.$$

Thus, $\eta' \sigma^{A \overset{\circ}{\omega}_2 C} \subseteq (\sigma\xi)^{B \overset{\circ}{\omega}_1 C}\eta'$ ($\subseteq$ because pr_1 of the left-hand side may be properly included in pr_1 of the right-hand side), and, consequently, $B \overset{\circ}{\omega}_1 C \geq A \overset{\circ}{\omega}_2 C$.

Assume that ξ is not one-to-one and let $\sigma_1, \ldots, \sigma_p \in \Sigma^A$ be such that $\sigma_1 \xi = \cdots = \sigma_p \xi$. Then by 5.7, $\sigma_1^A = \cdots = \sigma_p^A$. Add to Σ^B $p - 1$ inputs equal, as mappings of S^B, to $(\sigma_1 \xi)^B$. (Sometimes some of the existing equal inputs may be used.) Repeat this procedure for all subsets of Σ^A composed of elements having the same image under ξ. The semiautomaton $B_1 = (S^B, \Sigma^{B_1}, M^{B_1})$, where Σ^{B_1} is Σ^B extended as above, covers B. Clearly, $B_1 \geq A$, and for this covering a one-to-one mapping ξ can be chosen. By the above lemma, for every $A \mathring{\omega}_2 C$ there exists an ω_1 such that $B_1 \mathring{\omega}_1 C \geq A \mathring{\omega}_2 C$.

This is the modification of Lemma B to the case when ξ is not one-to-one. After coinciding the equal inputs in B_1 and B one obtains isomorphic semiautomata, and it is especially important for what follows that $G_{B_1} \simeq G_B$.

5.11 Covering with Cascade Product (the Partition Case)

In the sequel the following notations will be used:

$m(\pi)$ the maximal number of elements in a block of a decomposition π of a finite set S.

φ_π the natural mapping of S onto the blocks of a *partition* π of S:

$$s\varphi_\pi = H_i \Leftrightarrow s \in H_i$$

(as introduced in Section 5.9).

THEOREM.   Given a semiautomaton $A = (S^A, \Sigma, M^A)$ and an admissible partition $\pi = \{H_i\}$ of S^A, there exists a semiautomaton $D = (S^D, \Sigma^D, M^D)$ such that $|S^D| = m(\pi)$, and $C \circ D \geq A$, where $C = A/\pi$.

Proof. Obviously, one can find a partition $\tau = \{K_j\}$ of S^A such that $\pi\tau = \pi_{\text{iden}}$ of S^A and $|\tau| = m(\pi)$. ($|\tau|$ is the number of blocks in the partition τ.)

Let

$$S^D = \{\bar{K}_j\}$$

$$\Sigma^D = S^C \times \Sigma = \{\bar{H}_i\} \times \Sigma$$

and

$$\bar{K}_j(\bar{H}_i, \sigma)^D = \overline{(K_j \cap H_i)\sigma^A\varphi_\tau}. \qquad (8)$$

Notice that the right-hand side in the last equality may be empty (this will happen when $K_j \cap H_i = \phi$). In these cases $\bar{K}_j(\bar{H}_i, \sigma)^D$ can be chosen arbitrarily. Denote by $T^{C \circ D} \subseteq S^{C \circ D}$ the set of all pairs $(\bar{H}_i, \bar{K}_j)$ such that $H_i \cap K_j \neq \phi$.

η is the one-to-one mapping of $T^{C \circ D}$ onto S^A:

$$(\bar{H}_i, \bar{K}_j)\eta = H_i \cap K_j.$$

Now, for every element of $T^{C \circ D}$:

$$
\begin{aligned}
(\bar{H}_i, \bar{K}_j)\eta\sigma^A &= (H_i \cap K_j)\sigma^A \\
&= H_i\sigma^A\varphi_\pi \cap (H_i \cap K_j)\sigma^A\varphi_\tau \\
&= (\overline{H_i\sigma^A\varphi_\pi}, \overline{(H_i \cap K_j)\sigma^A\varphi_\tau})\eta \\
&= (\bar{H}_i\sigma^C, \bar{K}_j(\bar{H}_i, \sigma)^D)\eta \\
&= (\bar{H}_i, \bar{K}_j)\sigma^{C \circ D}\eta.
\end{aligned}
$$

This proves that $C \circ D \geq A$.

If τ is an *admissible* partition of S^A, then the mappings $(\bar{H}_i, \sigma)^D$ do not depend on $\bar{H}_i$, because all elements of K_j are mapped by σ^A into the same block of τ. All inputs in Σ^D with the same σ are equal, and after coinciding them, the cascade product $C \circ D$ reduces to the direct product $C \times D$.

5.12   Covering with Cascade Product (the Decomposition Case)

The construction in Section 5.8 allows the last result to be extended to the following important theorem:

THEOREM.   Let $A = (S^A, \Sigma, M^A)$ be a semiautomaton, π an admissible decomposition of S^A, and B a π-factor A/π of A. Then there exist semi-automata C and D such that $C \simeq B$ (C is isomorphic to B), $|S^D| = m(\pi)$, and $C^\circ D \geq A$.

Proof.   Using π and the given B, the semiautomaton A^* is constructed. π^* is an admissible partition of A^*; hence, as in the last theorem, there exists a D such that $C^\circ D \geq A^*$, where $C = A^*/\pi^*$ and $|S^D| = m(\pi^*)$. But $A^* \geq A$, $A^*/\pi^* \simeq A/\pi$, and $m(\pi^*) = m(\pi)$ (cf. the definition of π^*). The theorem follows.

EXAMPLE.

$$A = \left(\{1, 2, 3, 4, 5, 6\}, \{\sigma_0, \sigma_1\}, \right.$$

$$\left\{ \sigma_0^A = \begin{pmatrix} 1 & 2 & 3 & 4 & 5 & 6 \\ 3 & 1 & 2 & 1 & 3 & 5 \end{pmatrix}, \sigma_1^A = \begin{pmatrix} 1 & 2 & 3 & 4 & 5 & 6 \\ 4 & 5 & 3 & 3 & 3 & 3 \end{pmatrix} \right\} \right).$$

A can be conveniently defined using the table

A	1	2	3	4	5	6
σ_0	3	1	2	1	3	5
σ_1	4	5	3	3	3	3

and this form of description will also be used here for other semi-automata.

$$\pi = \{H_1 = \{1, 2, 3\}, H_2 = \{3, 4, 5\}, H_3 = \{5, 6\}\}$$

is an admissible decomposition of S^A. The following table defines a π-factor of A: $A/\pi = B$

B	$\bar{H}_1$	$\bar{H}_2$	$\bar{H}_3$
σ_0	$\bar{H}_1$	$\bar{H}_1$	$\bar{H}_2$
σ_1	$\bar{H}_2$	$\bar{H}_1$	$\bar{H}_1$

Notice that $\bar{H}_2\sigma_1^B$ and $\bar{H}_3\sigma_1^B$ can be defined both as $\bar{H}_1$ or $\bar{H}_2$; the particular choice is arbitrary.

The semiautomaton A^* is given by ($1\bar{H}_1$ will be written instead of $(1, \bar{H}_1)$, etc.):

A^*	$1\bar{H}_1$	$2\bar{H}_1$	$3\bar{H}_1$	$3\bar{H}_2$	$4\bar{H}_2$	$5\bar{H}_2$	$5\bar{H}_3$	$6\bar{H}_3$
σ_0	$3\bar{H}_1$	$1\bar{H}_1$	$2\bar{H}_1$	$2\bar{H}_1$	$1\bar{H}_1$	$3\bar{H}_1$	$3\bar{H}_2$	$5\bar{H}_2$
σ_1	$4\bar{H}_2$	$5\bar{H}_2$	$3\bar{H}_2$	$3\bar{H}_1$	$3\bar{H}_1$	$3\bar{H}_1$	$3\bar{H}_1$	$3\bar{H}_1$

The partition π^* is:

$$\pi^* = \{H_1^* = \{1\bar{H}_1, 2\bar{H}_1, 3\bar{H}_1\}, H_2^* =$$

$$\{3\bar{H}_2, 4\bar{H}_2, 5\bar{H}_2\}, H_3^* = \{5\bar{H}_3, 6\bar{H}_3\}\}.$$

The semiautomaton $C = A^*/\pi^*$ is

C	$\bar{H}_1^*$	$\bar{H}_2^*$	$\bar{H}_3^*$
σ_0	$\bar{H}_1^*$	$\bar{H}_1^*$	$\bar{H}_2^*$
σ_1	$\bar{H}_2^*$	$\bar{H}_1^*$	$\bar{H}_1^*$

C is isomorphic to B.

A partition τ of S^{A^*} has to be found such that $\pi^*\tau = \pi_{\text{iden}}$ of S^{A^*}. τ must have at least three blocks ($m(\pi^*) = 3$). One possibility is:

$$\tau = \{K_1 = \{1\bar{H}_1, 3\bar{H}_2, 5\bar{H}_3\}, K_2 = \{2\bar{H}_1, 4\bar{H}_2, 6\bar{H}_3\}, K_3 = \{3\bar{H}_1, 5\bar{H}_2\}\}.$$

The semiautomaton D is given by:

D	$\overline{K}_1$	$\overline{K}_2$	$\overline{K}_3$	
$(\overline{H}_1{}^*, \sigma_0)$	$\overline{K}_3$	$\overline{K}_1$	$\overline{K}_2$	
$(\overline{H}_1{}^*, \sigma_1)$	$\overline{K}_2$	$\overline{K}_3$	$\overline{K}_1$	
$(\overline{H}_2{}^*, \sigma_0)$	$\overline{K}_2$	$\overline{K}_1$	$\overline{K}_3$	
$(\overline{H}_2{}^*, \sigma_1)$	$\overline{K}_3$	$\overline{K}_3$	$\overline{K}_3$	
$(\overline{H}_3{}^*, \sigma_0)$	$\overline{K}_1$	$\overline{K}_3$	$\overline{K}_3$	$\longrightarrow$ arbitrarily
$(\overline{H}_3{}^*, \sigma_1)$	$\overline{K}_3$	$\overline{K}_3$	$\overline{K}_3$	

The semiautomaton $C{}^\circ D$ is

$C{}^\circ D$	a	b	c	d	e
	$(\overline{H}_1^*, \overline{K}_1)$	$(\overline{H}_1^*, \overline{K}_2)$	$(\overline{H}_1^*, \overline{K}_3)$	$(\overline{H}_2^*, \overline{K}_1)$	$(\overline{H}_2^*, \overline{K}_2)$
σ_0	$(\overline{H}_1^*, \overline{K}_3)$	$(\overline{H}_1^*, \overline{K}_1)$	$(\overline{H}_1^*, \overline{K}_2)$	$(\overline{H}_1^*, \overline{K}_2)$	$(\overline{H}_1^*, \overline{K}_1)$
σ_1	$(\overline{H}_2^*, \overline{K}_2)$	$(\overline{H}_2^*, \overline{K}_3)$	$(\overline{H}_2^*, \overline{K}_1)$	$(\overline{H}_1^*, \overline{K}_3)$	$(\overline{H}_1^*, \overline{K}_3)$

$C{}^\circ D$	f	g	h	k
	$(\overline{H}_2^*, \overline{K}_3)$	$(\overline{H}_3^*, \overline{K}_1)$	$(\overline{H}_3^*, \overline{K}_2)$	$(\overline{H}_3^*, \overline{K}_3)$
σ_0	$(\overline{H}_1^*, \overline{K}_3)$	$(\overline{H}_2^*, \overline{K}_1)$	$(\overline{H}_2^*, \overline{K}_3)$	$(\overline{H}_2^*, \overline{K}_3)$
σ_1	$(\overline{H}_1^*, \overline{K}_3)$	$(\overline{H}_1^*, \overline{K}_3)$	$(\overline{H}_1^*, \overline{K}_3)$	$(\overline{H}_1^*, \overline{K}_3)$

Checking of the fact that $C{}^\circ D \geq A$:

$C{}^\circ D \geq A^*$ by the mapping (the elements of $S^{C{}^\circ D}$ are redenoted as in the above table):

$$\eta_1 = \begin{pmatrix} a & b & c & d & e & f & g & h \\ 1\overline{H}_1 & 2\overline{H}_1 & 3\overline{H}_1 & 3\overline{H}_2 & 4\overline{H}_2 & 5\overline{H}_2 & 5\overline{H}_3 & 6\overline{H}_3 \end{pmatrix}.$$

Notice that $T^{C{}^\circ D} = S^{C{}^\circ D} - \{(\overline{H}_3^*, \overline{K}_3)\}$.

$A^* \geq A$ by the mapping

$$\eta_2 = \begin{pmatrix} 1\bar{H}_1 & 2\bar{H}_1 & 3\bar{H}_1 & 3\bar{H}_2 & 4\bar{H}_2 & 5\bar{H}_2 & 5\bar{H}_3 & 6\bar{H}_3 \\ 1 & 2 & 3 & 3 & 4 & 5 & 5 & 6 \end{pmatrix}.$$

Hence, $C°D \geq A$ by the mapping

$$\eta = \eta_1\eta_2 = \begin{pmatrix} a & b & c & d & e & f & g & h \\ 1 & 2 & 3 & 3 & 4 & 5 & 5 & 6 \end{pmatrix}.$$

Indeed, for σ_0 one has:

$$\eta\sigma_0^A = \begin{pmatrix} a & b & c & d & e & f & g & h \\ 3 & 1 & 2 & 2 & 1 & 3 & 3 & 5 \end{pmatrix} = \sigma_0^{C°D}\eta$$

and for σ_1:

$$\eta\sigma_1^A = \begin{pmatrix} a & b & c & d & e & f & g & h \\ 4 & 5 & 3 & 3 & 3 & 3 & 3 & 3 \end{pmatrix} = \sigma_1^{C°D}\eta.$$

Chapter 6

Covering by Permutation and Reset Semiautomata

6.1 Permutation-Reset Semiautomata

Consider the semiautomaton $A = (S^A, \Sigma, M^A)$ with $|S^A| = n$, and let π be the decomposition of S^A, the blocks of which are all subsets of S^A having exactly $n - 1$ elements. For every $S \subseteq S^A$ and every $\sigma \in \Sigma$, $|S\sigma^A| \leq |S|$; hence, π is an admissible decomposition. It can be used to construct a π-factor $A/\pi = B$ of a very special nature [18].

Suppose $|S^A\sigma^A| < n$, then there exists an $H_i \in \pi$ such that $S^A\sigma^A \subseteq H_i$; consequently, for every $H_j \in \pi$:

$$H_j\sigma^A \subseteq S^A\sigma^A \subseteq H_i.$$

Define $\overline{H_j\sigma^B} = \overline{H_i}$ for all j; i.e., σ^B maps all elements of S^B onto one element (i.e., $|pr_2\sigma^B| = 1$). An input having this property will be called a *reset input*.

If $|S^A\sigma^A| = n$, σ^A is a permutation of S^A. Then for every H_i there exists exactly one H_j such that $H_i\sigma^A \subseteq H_j$, actually $H_i\sigma^A = H_j$. In this case $H_i \neq H_j \Rightarrow H_i\sigma^A \neq H_j\sigma^A$ is also true, i.e., σ^A permutes not only the elements of S^A but also the blocks of π, and σ^B necessarily will be a permutation of S^B. An input in a semiautomaton which permutes its states is called a *permutation input*.

123

All inputs in the π-factor B constructed as above are either reset or permutation inputs—a semiautomaton with this property is called a *permutation-reset semiautomaton.*

Using the theorem in Section 5.12 one can now cover A by a cascade product $C°D$ in which C is a permutation-reset semiautomaton and $|S^D| = n - 1$. The same construction is then applied to D, which can be covered by a cascade product $E°F$, where E is a permutation-reset semiautomaton and $|S^F| = n - 2$. By Lemma A in 5.10, $C°(E°F) \geq C°D$, i.e., $C°(E°F) \geq A$. By repeating this construction one obtains the following theorem:

THEOREM.   Every semiautomaton with $n \geq 2$ states can be covered by a cascade product of at most $n - 1$ permutation-reset semiautomata.

The number $n - 1$ in the theorem results from the observation that every two-state semiautomaton is necessarily a permutation-reset one.

6.2   Permutation and Reset Semiautomata

DEFINITION.   A *permutation semiautomaton A* is a semiautomaton in which σ^A is a permutation of S^A for every $\sigma \in \Sigma^A$.

A *reset semiautomaton A* is a semiautomaton in which σ^A $(\sigma \in \Sigma^A)$ is either an identity on S^A or $|S^A\sigma^A| = 1$.

The following will now be proved:

THEOREM.   Every permutation-reset semiautomaton A can be covered by a cascade product $C°D$ of a permutation semiautomaton C and a reset semiautomaton D.

Proof. $\Sigma^A = \Sigma$ can be divided into two disjoint subsets:

$$\Sigma = \Sigma_p \cup \Sigma_r \qquad (\Sigma_p \cap \Sigma_r = \phi),$$

where $\Sigma_p = \{\sigma_p\}$ is the set of all permutation inputs of A, and $\Sigma_r = \{\sigma_r\}$ is the set of all reset inputs of A. Let $\bar{G}_A$ be the subgroup of G_A generated by the permutations $\{\sigma_p^A\}_{\sigma_p \in \Sigma_p}$. The elements of $\bar{G}_A$, i.e., the *distinct* permutations x_p^A, where $x_p \in \Sigma_p^*$, will form the states of C, and in this role they will be denoted by $\overline{x_p^A}$. $\Sigma^C = \Sigma$, and M^C is defined as follows:

$$\overline{x_p^A}\sigma_p^C = \overline{x_p^A \sigma_p^A} = \overline{(x\sigma)_p^A}, \qquad \overline{x_p^A}\sigma_r^C = \overline{x_p^A}.$$

Thus, C is a permutation semiautomaton.

Let

$$S^D = \{\overline{s^A}\}_{s^A \in S^A},$$

$$\Sigma^D = S^C \times \Sigma,$$

and

$$\overline{s^A}(\overline{x_p^A}, \sigma_p)^D = \overline{s^A}, \qquad \overline{s^A}(\overline{x_p^A}, \sigma_r)^D = \overline{(s^A\sigma_r^A)(x_p^A)^{-1}}.$$

$s^A\sigma_r^A$ is the same for all s^A; hence, D is a reset semiautomaton.

$C \circ D \geq A$: let η be a mapping of $S^{C \circ D}$ into S^A defined by

$$(\overline{x_p^A}, \overline{s^A})\eta = s^A x_p^A,$$

and as x_p^A is a permutation of S^A, η is a mapping of $S^{C \circ D}$ onto S^A. Now

$$(\overline{x_p^A}, \overline{s^A})\eta \sigma_p^A = s^A x_p^A \sigma_p^A = s^A(x\sigma)_p^A = ((\overline{x\sigma)_p^A}, \overline{s^A})\eta$$

$$= (\overline{x_p^A}\sigma_p^C, \overline{s^A}(\overline{x_p^A}, \sigma_p)^D)\eta = (\overline{x_p^A}, \overline{s^A})\sigma_p^{C \circ D}\eta$$

and

$$(\overline{x_p^A}, \overline{s^A})\eta \sigma_r^A = s^A x_p^A \sigma_r^A = s^A \sigma_r^A$$

$$= (s^A\sigma_r^A)(x_p^A)^{-1}x_p^A$$

$$= (\overline{x_p^A}, \overline{(s^A\sigma_r^A)(x_p^A)^{-1}})\eta$$

$$= (\overline{x_p^A}\sigma_r^C, \overline{s^A}(\overline{x_p^A}, \sigma_r)^D)\eta$$

$$= (\overline{x_p^A}, \overline{s^A})\sigma_r^{C \circ D}\eta.$$

6.3   Covering of Reset Semiautomata

In a reset semiautomaton A every partition of S^A is admissible, because σ^A is either the identity or maps S^A onto a singleton. Hence, A (with $|S^A| \geq 2$) can always be covered by a direct product $B \times C$, where $|S^B| = 2$ and $|S^C| < |S^A|$. Indeed, take any partition π of S^A having two blocks: obviously $m(\pi) < |S^A|$, and the above follows immediately.

By applying the same procedure to C, and observing that

$$B \times C \geq A, \qquad D \times E \geq C \Rightarrow B \times (D \times E) = B \times D \times E \geq A$$

one obtains the following theorem:

THEOREM.   Every reset semiautomaton can be covered by a direct product of two-state reset semiautomata.

6.4   Grouplike Semiautomata

Consider the permutation semiautomaton C from Section 6.2. The states of C are the elements of a group $\bar{G}_A$ (henceforth in this chapter denoted by G) of permutations of S^A. Every mapping of the states of C due to an input is a right translation (i.e., multiplying from right) by one of these permutations (i.e., by an element of G; e.g., for the reset inputs this is the identity element). It follows that if a semiautomaton $G = (S^G, \Sigma^G, M^G)$ is defined with:

$$S^G = G, \quad \Sigma^G = G \quad \text{and} \quad g_1 g_2^G = g_1 g_2 \qquad (g_1, g_2 \in G)$$

then $G \geq C$. (Indeed, in Section 5.7 put for η the identity mapping of $S^G = G$ onto $S^C = G$, and for ξ the mapping of Σ^C into $\Sigma^G = G$ taking every $\sigma \in \Sigma^C$ onto that element of G which performs the same right translation as σ^C.)

A semiautomaton $G = (G, \Sigma^G, M^G)$ in which G is a group and σ^G ($\sigma \in \Sigma^G$) are right translations of G (each such translation appearing at least once) will be called a *grouplike semiautomaton,* and the above can be expressed by saying that the semiautomaton C from 6.2 can be covered by a group like semiautomaton G. Moreover, and this observation will be useful in the next chapter, *the group G is isomorphic to the group $\bar{G}_A$ generated by the permutation inputs of the permutation-reset semiautomaton A, which is covered by $C \circ D$ in 6.2.*

6.5   Covering of Grouplike Semiautomata

Given a grouplike semiautomaton $G = (G, G, M^G)$, assume that the group G has a subgroup $H = \{e, h_2, \ldots, h_t\}$ (e is the identity of G). Let π be the partition of G into right cosets of H:

$$\pi = \{H, Hk_2, Hk_3, \ldots, Hk_u\}$$

where $K = \{e, k_2, k_3, \ldots, k_u\}$ is a set of representatives of the distinct cosets of H. (Notice that $tu = |G|$.) π is an admissible partition of G, considered as a semiautomaton; π induces only a right congruence on G considered as a group, but in the semiautomaton G the action of an input is actually multiplication from *the right* by a group element. Formally, for every $i = 1, \ldots, u$ and every $g \in G$,

$$Hk_i g^G = Hk_i g = Hk_j \qquad \text{for some } j.$$

The union of the subsets of G in $\tau = \{K, h_2K, \ldots, h_tK\}$ has at most $|G|$ distinct elements, but as

$$K \cup h_2K \cup \cdots \cup h_tK = HK$$

$$= H \cup Hk_2 \cup \cdots \cup Hk_u = G,$$

it has exactly $|G|$ distinct elements. Every subset in τ has at most u distinct elements, there are t such subsets, $ut = |G|$; hence, τ is a partition of G. Next, observe that $\pi\tau = \pi_{\text{iden}}$ of G. Indeed,

$Hk_i \cap h_j K = \{h_j k_i\}$, because otherwise there will be a $k_m \neq k_i$ such that $Hk_m \cap Hk_i \neq \phi$, which is impossible (the k's are representatives of distinct cosets). At the same time every $g \in G$ can be written in the form $h_j k_i$, and so the above assertion is verified.

The theorem from Section 5.11 can be applied (using π and τ) to cover G by $G/\pi^\circ D$. Especially interesting is the fact that after coinciding equal inputs in D one obtains a semiautomaton isomorphic to the grouplike semiautomaton

$$H = (H, H, M^H).$$

To this end, let η be the one-to-one mapping of H onto S^D defined by $h_i \eta = \overline{h_i K}$.

For every $k_j \in K$ and every $g \in G$ the product $k_j g$ belongs exactly to one block of τ, i.e., to some $h_n K$. In other words, there is a unique $k_m \in K$ and a unique h_n such that $k_j g = h_n k_m$. Define the mapping ξ of Σ^D into $\Sigma^H = H$ by $(\overline{Hk_j}, g)\xi = h_n$, where h_n is as defined above. ξ is, clearly, a mapping onto H because by changing g and k_j all blocks of τ can be obtained.

Now it will be proved that $\eta(\overline{Hk_j}, g)^D = ((\overline{Hk_j}, g)\xi)^H \eta$. Indeed, for every $h_i \in H$:

$$h_i \eta (\overline{Hk_j}, g)^D = \overline{h_i K}(\overline{Hk_j}, g)^D = \overline{(h_i K \cap Hk_j)g^G \varphi_\tau}$$

$$= \overline{(h_i k_j)g^G \varphi_\tau} = \overline{(h_i k_j g)\varphi_\tau} = \overline{(h_i h_n k_m)\varphi_\tau}$$

$$= \overline{h_i h_n K} = (h_i h_n)\eta = h_i((\overline{Hk_j}, g)\xi)^H \eta.$$

The situation is exactly as in the corollary of Lemma A in 5.7; hence, coinciding the equal inputs in D will result in a semiautomaton D_1 isomorphic to the grouplike semiautomaton H. If the above ξ is taken as ω one obtains the following theorem:

THEOREM A.   Let G be a grouplike semiautomaton and H a subgroup of G. G can be covered by a cascade product $C \dot\omega D_1$ such that the semiautomaton D_1 is also a grouplike semiautomaton isomorphic to H.

For H a *normal* subgroup of G, π induces a congruence on G, i.e., π

is an admissible partition of G considered both as a semiautomaton and as a group. If g_1 and g_2 belong to the same coset of H in G, then in the π-factor $B = G/\pi$, g_1^B and g_2^B will be equal. B is a grouplike semiautomaton with a group ismorphic to G/H. Using this observation and Theorem A one proves, by an argument analogous to that in 6.1:

THEOREM B.   Let G be a grouplike semiautomaton and $G = H_0, H_1,$ $\ldots, H_k = \{e\}$ a *normal series* of G (that is, every H_i is a proper normal subgroup of H_{i-1}; e is the identity in G). Then G can be covered by a cascade product of grouplike semiautomata with groups isomorphic to the factors H_{i-1}/H_i of the given series.

Every finite group has, clearly, a *composition series*, i.e., a normal series in which every factor H_{i-1}/H_i is a simple group.

Thus, a grouplike semiautomaton can be covered by a cascade product of *simple grouplike semiautomata*—i.e., ones which correspond to simple groups.

6.6 Covering by Simple Grouplike and Two-State Reset Semiautomata

The distinct constructions done in this chapter can be combined (using the lemmas in 5.10) to give the following theorem:

THEOREM.   Every semiautomaton A can be covered by direct and cascade products of semiautomata of two kinds:

(a) simple grouplike semiautomata,
(b) two-state reset semiautomata.

This theorem is a part of a theorem by Krohn and Rhodes which will be presented in the next chapter.

Chapter 7

The Theory of Krohn and Rhodes

7.1 The Main Theorem

The following theorem belongs to K. B. Krohn and J. L. Rhodes [22, 23]:

THEOREM.   Every semiautomaton A can be covered by direct and cascade products of semiautomata of two kinds:

(a)   simple grouplike semiautomata with simple groups which are homomorphic images of subgroups of the semigroup G_A of A;

(b)   two-state reset semiautomata.

Everything but the result about the possibility of allowing simple groups from a certain "origin" only was proved in the previous chapter. Here a modification of a construction of P. H. Zeiger [48, 49] will be used to complete the proof.

The grouplike semiautomata used to cover A were obtained in three steps:

(a) A was covered by a cascade product of permutation-reset semiautomata.

(b)   Every such permutation-reset semiautomaton was covered by a cascade product of a permutation semiautomaton and a reset semiautomaton.

(c) The obtained permutation semiautomaton was covered by a cascade product of simple grouplike semiautomata.

The simple groups appearing in (c) are homomorphic images of subgroups of the group of the permutation semiautomaton obtained in (b). This group is the group generated by the permutation inputs of the corresponding permutation-reset semiautomaton obtained in (a).

Thus, the crucial step is the first one, and the theorem will be proved if it is shown that every semiautomaton A can be covered by a cascade product of permutation-reset semiautomata such that the subgroups of their semigroups, generated by their permutation inputs, are homomorphic images of subgroups of G_A. This will be achieved by constructing series of admissible decompositions of S^A having special properties.

7.2 Construction of Special Admissible Decompositions

Let π be an admissible decomposition of S^A and assume $m(\pi) > 1$. Let $A/\pi = B$ be a π-factor of A.

Among the blocks of π having $m(\pi)$ elements (i.e., the largest blocks of π), it is always possible to find a subset, say $\pi_m = \{H_1, \ldots, H_m\}$, such that

$$H_i, H_j \in \pi_m \Rightarrow \exists\, x_1, x_2 \in \Sigma^*, \quad H_i x_1^A = H_j, \quad H_j x_2^A = H_i \quad (\Sigma = \Sigma^A)$$

and no x^A maps a block not in π_m onto a block in π_m.

The existence of at least one such subset π_m follows from the fact that the identity mapping $\wedge^A$ maps every block onto itself, and the relation between blocks belonging to a π_m is transitive (since if $H_i x^A = H_j$ and $H_j y^A = H_k$, then $H_i (xy)^A = H_k$).

For a set of sets $\{u_j\}$, $\max(\{u_j\})$ will denote the set of all distinct sets in $\{u_j\}$ maximal under inclusion.

Consider the following subsets of S^A:

$\pi' = $ the subsets $\{H\}_{H \in \pi - \pi_m}$ and the subsets in each

$$\max(\{Hx^A\}_{\substack{H \in \pi \\ x \in \Sigma^* \\ Hx^A \subseteq H_i}} \cup \{s^A\}_{s^A \in H_i} - \{H_i\}) \qquad \text{for } i = 1, 2, \ldots, m$$

$$= \pi_1' \text{ and } \pi_2' \quad (9)$$

Here $\pi_1' = \{H\}_{H \in \pi - \pi_m}$ contains all blocks in π which are not in π_m, and π_2' contains the subsets of S^A obtained by applying the max operation to the expressions in the brackets independently for every i ($i = 1, 2, \ldots, m$). Notice that more than one copy of a subset of S^A may appear in π_1' and/or in π_2' (such copies must be distinctly labeled); for this reason the word description rather than the sign $\cup$ (set theoretical union) was used in (9).

π' is a decomposition of S^A, because all elements of S^A which are not in blocks of π_m appear in some other blocks of π, and the elements of S^A in the blocks of π_m are, obviously, taken care of by the blocks of π_2'.

π' is *properly* finer than π ($\pi' < \pi$) in the sense that the blocks in π_m of π are "replaced" in π' by smaller ones.

Finally, π' is an admissible decomposition of S^A. Indeed, for every block H' of π' and every $\sigma \in \Sigma$, $H'\sigma^A$ is included either in a block of $\pi - \pi_m$, or it is a proper subset of a block in π_m, which will, clearly, be included in a block of π_2'. Notice that $H_i \in \pi_m$ can be an image (onto) of a block $H_j \in \pi_m$ only, but *all* these blocks are deleted.

7.3   Properties of the Constructed Decomposition

The blocks of π_2' included in $H_i \in \pi_m$ will be denoted by

$$H_{i1}, H_{i2}, \ldots, H_{i\alpha_i}.$$

For every $H_i \in \pi_m$ there exists a $y_i \in \Sigma^*$ such that $H_i y_i = H_1$. (In this section the mappings x^A will be denoted simply by x—all mappings here refer to the semiautomaton A.)

There exists, also, at least one $x_i \in \Sigma^*$ such that $H_1 x_i = H_i$. Hence, $H_1 x_i y_i = H_1$, i.e., $x_i y_i$ is a permutation of the elements in H_1, and for some n the permutation $(x_i y_i)^n$ will be the identity on H_1. $(x_i y_i)^{n-1} x_i$ maps H_1 onto H_i, hence the block H_{1p} into, say, H_{iq} (notice that π_2' is an admissible decomposition of the set of elements of S^A in π_m, with respect to all maps taking blocks of π_m into such blocks). Now:

$$H_{1p} = H_{1p}(x_i y_i)^n = H_{1p}(x_i y_i)^{n-1} x_i y_i \subseteq H_{iq} y_i,$$

and, as y_i maps H_i onto H_1, there exists an H_{1r} such that $H_{iq} y_i \subseteq H_{1r}$. The maximality of the blocks of π_2' included in H_1 implies that

$$H_{1p} = H_{1r} = H_{iq} y_i.$$

y_i is a one-to-one mapping, hence, $|H_{1p}| = |H_{iq}|$, and since, also, $(x_i y_i)^{n-1} x_i$ is one-to-one, $H_{1p}(x_i y_i)^{n-1} x_i = H_{iq}$.

For $H_{1p_1} \neq H_{1p}$, the same reasoning gives $H_{1p_1}(x_i y_i)^{n-1} x_i = H_{iq_1}$ with $H_{iq_1} \neq H_{iq}$, because otherwise the mapping $(x_i y_i)^{n-1} x_i$ would take $H_{1p} \cup H_{1p_1}$ onto H_{iq}, while

$$|H_{1p} \cup H_{1p_1}| > |H_{1p}| = |H_{iq}|.$$

Altogether, $(x_i y_i)^{n-1} x_i$ maps distinct blocks of π_2' in H_1 onto distinct blocks of π_2' in H_i. The roles of H_1 and H_i can be interchanged, hence the conclusion: all H_i in π_m have the same number of blocks of π_2', i.e.,

$$\alpha_1 = \alpha_2 = \cdots = \alpha_m = \alpha.$$

Enumerate arbitrarily the blocks of π_2' in H_1, and then enumerate the blocks of π_2' in every H_i ($i = 2, \ldots, m$) so that the above mapping $(x_i y_i)^{n-1} x_i$ will map H_{1p} onto H_{ip}; hence, also, $H_{ip} y_i = H_{1p}$.

Assume that for some $\sigma \in \Sigma$ there exist H_i and H_j in π_m such that $H_i \sigma = H_j$. Analogous to the above y_i this σ must map distinct blocks $H_{i1}, \ldots, H_{i\alpha}$ onto distinct blocks $H_{j1}, \ldots, H_{j\alpha}$. This mapping can be described as a permutation γ_σ^{ij} of the (second) indices $1, 2, \ldots, \alpha$.

If $p\gamma_\sigma^{ij} = q$ (i.e., $H_{ip}\sigma = H_{jq}$), one obtains (with x_i, y_i as above and an analogous y_j)

$$H_{1p}(x_i y_i)^{n-1} x_i \sigma y_j = H_{ip}\sigma y_j = H_{jq} y_j = H_{1q}.$$

Consequently, the mapping $(x_i y_i)^{n-1} x_i \sigma y_j$ (which depends only on i, j, and σ, but not on p and q) permutes the blocks $H_{11}, \ldots, H_{1\alpha}$ exactly as γ_σ^{ij} permutes the indices $1, 2, \ldots, \alpha$. This observation will be of great importance in the sequel.

7.4   The Corresponding Semiautomaton

Arrange the blocks of π' in the following array:

	L_1	L_2	$\ldots$	L_α
K_1	$\overline{H}_{11}$	$\overline{H}_{12}$	$\ldots$	$\overline{H}_{1\alpha}$
K_2	$\overline{H}_{21}$	$\overline{H}_{22}$	$\ldots$	$\overline{H}_{2\alpha}$
$\vdots$	$\vdots$	$\vdots$		$\vdots$
K_m	$\overline{H}_{m1}$	$\overline{H}_{m2}$	$\ldots$	$\overline{H}_{m\alpha}$
K_{m+1}	$\overline{H}_{m+1}$			
$\vdots$	$\vdots$			
K_t	$\overline{H}_t$			

The H_{ij}'s are defined in Section 7.3, and $H_{m+1}, \ldots, H_t$ are the blocks in π_1'. The bars indicate that all blocks are considered now as elements of the set of states S^F of a π'-factor of A, F, which will be defined as follows:

First, $\Sigma^F = \Sigma^A$. Now, to define M^F notice that the set of elements of S^A in all blocks of π' appearing in the row i of the array is exactly H_i. If $H_i\sigma^A \notin \pi_m$, one consults the π-factor $B = A/\pi$, and finds there $\overline{H}_i\sigma^B = \overline{H}_j$. This means that $H_i\sigma^A \subseteq H_j$, and by the construction of (9) there necessarily exists a block of π' in the row j including $H_i\sigma^A$. The corresponding element of S^F (it is in K_j, of course) will be defined as the image under σ^F of all elements of S^F in K_i.

Now consider the case where $H_i\sigma^A = H_j \in \pi_m$. This is possible only if $H_i \in \pi_m$, also. Since there may be blocks in π included one in the other, and, in particular, equal blocks, there may be several blocks in π_m equal to $H_i\sigma^A$; then take for H_j that one for which $\overline{H}_i\sigma^B = \overline{H}_j$ in B. σ^F is defined to map the elements of K_i onto those of K_j, exactly as σ^A maps the corresponding blocks of π_2' in H_i onto the blocks of π_2' in H_j, according to 7.3.

Let ρ denote the partition of S^F into the subsets $K_1, K_2, \ldots, K_t$. The above definition of M^F ensures that ρ is an admissible partition of S^F, and, moreover, $C = F/\rho$ is isomorphic to $B = A/\pi$.

7.5   Covering of the Constructed Semiautomaton

The partition of S^F into the subsets $L_1, L_2, \ldots, L_\alpha$ (the columns of the array in 7.4) will be denoted by τ. Evidently, $\rho\tau = \pi_{\text{iden}}$ of S^F. As in Section 5.11, a semiautomaton D with states which are the blocks of τ will be constructed, and $C^\circ D \geq F$.

Now it will be shown that D can be made a permutation-reset semiautomaton. The inputs of D are of the form (K_i, σ), and as in 5.11

$$\bar{L}_k(\bar{K}_i, \sigma)^D = \overline{(L_k \cap K_i)\sigma^F \varphi_\tau}.$$

If i is one of the numbers $m + 1, m + 2, \ldots, t$, only $L_1 \cap K_i \neq \phi$; and for all $k = 1, 2, \ldots, \alpha$ define

$$\bar{L}_k(\bar{K}_i, \sigma)^D = \bar{L}_1(\bar{K}_i, \sigma)^D,$$

i.e., $(\bar{K}_i, \sigma)$ is a reset input in D.

If $i \in \{1, 2, \ldots, m\}$ and $H_i \sigma^A \notin \pi_m$, then by the construction of F in 7.4 all elements of K_i will have the same image in F under σ^F, i.e., $\bar{L}_k(\bar{K}_i, \sigma)^D$ will not depend on k, and $(\bar{K}_i, \sigma)$ is once more a reset input.

The last possibility is that $i \in \{1, 2, \ldots, m\}$ and $H_i \sigma^A = H_j \in \pi_m$. Then, by definition of σ^F, one obtains:

$$\bar{L}_k(\bar{K}_i, \sigma)^D = \overline{(L_k \cap K_i)\sigma^F \varphi_\tau} = \overline{\bar{H}_{ik}\sigma^F \varphi_\tau}$$

$$= \overline{\bar{H}_{j,k\gamma_\sigma^{ij}}\varphi_\tau} = \bar{L}_{k\gamma_\sigma^{ij}}$$

i.e., $(\bar{K}_i, \sigma)$ permutes the states of D (i.e., $\bar{L}_1, \ldots, \bar{L}_\alpha$) exactly in the same way as γ_σ^{ij} permutes the indices $1, 2, \ldots, \alpha$. Thus, $(\bar{K}_i, \sigma)$ is a permutation input, and D is a permutation-reset semiautomaton.

7.6   The Properties of the Constructed Covering

It follows from Sections 7.5 and 7.3 that to every permutation input of D there corresponds a $x \in \Sigma^*$ such that x^A permutes $H_{11}, H_{12}, \ldots, H_{1\alpha}$

exactly in the same way as the above input permutes the states of D: $\bar{L}_1, \bar{L}_2, \ldots, \bar{L}_\alpha$. Hence, the subgroup of G_D, generated by all permutation inputs of D, is isomorphic to the group of permutations of the subsets of S^A: $H_{11}, \ldots, H_{1\alpha}$, generated by the corresponding $x^A \in G_A$, when restricted to the above subsets and considered as permutations of these subsets.

In order to prove that this group is a homomorphic image of a subgroup of G_A consider Theorem C from Section 1.16. It cannot be applied directly to the present situation because permutations of, in general, overlapping subsets of S^A appear here instead of elements of S^A. To handle this case, consider the set $S = S^A \cup S^0$, where $S^0 = \{H_{11}, \ldots, H_{1\alpha}\}$: To every z^A ($z \in \Sigma^*$), which permutes the above subsets, put in correspondence a mapping $\bar{z}$ of S into S, which coincides with z^A on S^A, and permutes the elements of S^0 exactly in the same way as z^A permutes the subsets with the same names. Clearly,

$$z_1^A = z_2^A \Leftrightarrow \bar{z}_1 = \bar{z}_2;$$

i.e., the subsemigroup G'_A of G_A generated by the z^A's is isomorphic to the semigroup $\bar{G}$ generated by the $\bar{z}$'s. Now the above theorem can be applied to obtain the result that the group generated by the said permutations of the elements S^0 of S is a homomorphic image of a subgroup of $\bar{G}$. It follows that the group of permutations of $\{H_{11}, \ldots, H_{1\alpha}\}$, generated by the x^A's (which correspond to the permutation inputs of D), restricted to $H_1 \subseteq S^A$, is a homomorphic image of a subgroup of G'_A, hence, of a subgroup of G_A.

The following theorem summarizes the entire development.

THEOREM.   Given a semiautomaton A and an admissible decomposition π of S^A with a π-factor $B = A/\pi$, one can find a properly finer decomposition π' of S^A and a π'-factor $F = A/\pi'$ such that F can be covered by a cascade product $C \circ D$, where $C \simeq B$, D is a permutation-reset semiautomaton, and the group generated by the permutation inputs in D is a homomorphic image of a subgroup of the semigroup G_A of A.

7.7 The Proof of the Main Theorem

To prove the theorem by Krohn and Rhodes (Section 7.1) start with the trivial decomposition π, where all elements of S^A form one block. $D_0 = A/\pi$ is a one-state semiautomaton, and so it is, clearly, a reset one. Find as above $\pi' < \pi$, and obtain $A/\pi' \leq D_0°D_1$, with D_1 having the properties mentioned in Section 7.6. Next, find by the same procedure $\pi'' < \pi'$, and obtain $A/\pi'' \leq A/\pi'°D_2$, with D_2 as in 7.6. Now use Lemma B from 5.10 (in all coverings here ξ is the identity) and obtain $A/\pi'' \leq (D_0°D_1)\overset{\circ}{\omega}D_2$.

This procedure is continued, and, since at every step the number of *maximal* blocks is reduced, after a finite number of steps, a decomposition $\pi^{(k)}$ of S^A will be obtained in which every block is a singleton. (It is possible, of course, that distinct blocks will actually be the same singleton.)

Thus, the semiautomaton $E = A/\pi^{(k)}$ is covered by a cascade product of permutation-reset semiautomata such that the subgroups of their semigroups, generated by their permutation inputs, are homomorphic images of subgroups of the semigroup G_A. The proof will be completed if it is shown that $E \geq A$. To this end, define the mapping η of S^E into S^A such that every element of S^E, i.e., every block of $\pi^{(k)}$, will be mapped by η onto the corresponding element of S^A. (The blocks of $\pi^{(k)}$ are singletons!) Clearly, η is onto, and for every $\sigma \in \Sigma^A = \Sigma^E$, $\eta\sigma^A = \sigma^E\eta$. Indeed, $E = A/\pi^{(k)}$, where $\pi^{(k)}$ is an admissible decomposition of S^A, hence, if for some s^E and σ, $s^E\sigma^E = s_1^E$, then the singleton s^A in the block of $\pi^{(k)}$ corresponding to s^E ($s^A = s^E\eta$) must be transformed by σ^A onto the singleton s_1^A, which forms the block corresponding to s_1^E ($s_1^A = s_1^E\eta$). Thus, $s^A\sigma^A = s_1^A$, and

$$s^E\eta\sigma^A = s^A\sigma^A = s_1^A = s_1^E\eta = s^E\sigma^E\eta.$$

7.8 Example

The above construction is applied to the semiautomaton

A	1	2	3	4	5	6
σ_0	3	1	2	1	3	5
σ_1	4	5	3	3	3	3

(a)   Let $\pi = \{H_1 = \{123456\}\}$ be the trivial decomposition of S^A and $B = A/\pi$ the π-factor

B	$\bar{H}_1$
σ_0	$\bar{H}_1$
σ_1	$\bar{H}_1$

$\pi_1 = \{H_1\}$ will serve as the π_m from Section 7.2.
   Using (9),

$$\pi' = \{H_{11} = \{1235\}, H_{12} = \{345\}, H_{13} =: \{6\}\}$$

is constructed. As in Section 7.4, one arranges the blocks of π':

	L_1	L_2	L_3
K_1	$\bar{H}_{11}$	$\bar{H}_{12}$	$\bar{H}_{13}$

They form the set of states S^{F_1} of a π'-factor of A, $A/\pi' = F_1$, which, according to 7.4, is defined by:

F_1	$\bar{H}_{11}$	$\bar{H}_{12}$	$\bar{H}_{13}$
σ_0	$\bar{H}_{11}$	$\bar{H}_{11}$	$\bar{H}_{11}$
σ_1	$\bar{H}_{12}$	$\bar{H}_{12}$	$\bar{H}_{12}$

As in Sections 7.4 and 7.5, the semiautomata

C_1	$\bar{K}_1$	D_1	$\bar{L}_1$	$\bar{L}_2$	$\bar{L}_3$
σ_0	$\bar{K}_1,$	$(\bar{K}_1, \sigma_0)$	$\bar{L}_1$	$\bar{L}_1$	$\bar{L}_1$
σ_1	$\bar{K}_1$	$(\bar{K}_1, \sigma_1)$	$\bar{L}_2$	$\bar{L}_2$	$\bar{L}_2$

are constructed. C_1 is isomorphic to $B = A/\pi$, D_1 is a reset semiautomaton, and $C_1{}^\circ D_1 \geq F_1$.

(b)   Now, one starts with the decomposition

$$\pi' = \{H_1 = \{1235\}, H_2 = \{345\}, H_3 = \{6\}\}$$

(the blocks are renamed for convenience) and with $F_1 = A/\pi'$:

F_1	$\bar{H}_1$	$\bar{H}_2$	$\bar{H}_3$
σ_0	$\bar{H}_1$	$\bar{H}_1$	$\bar{H}_1$
σ_1	$\bar{H}_2$	$\bar{H}_2$	$\bar{H}_2$

Here $\pi_m = \pi_1 = \{H_1 = \{1235\}\}$ and by (9):

$$\pi'' = \{H_2 = \{345\}, H_3 = \{6\}, H_{11} = \{123\}, H_{12} = \{5\}\}.$$

The blocks

	L_1	L_2
K_1	$\bar{H}_{11}$	$\bar{H}_{12}$
K_2	$\bar{H}_2$	
K_3	$\bar{H}_3$	

form the set of states S^{F_2} of a π''-factor of A, $A/\pi'' = F_2$, which is given by

F_2	$\bar{H}_{11}$	$\bar{H}_{12}$	$\bar{H}_2$	$\bar{H}_3$
σ_0	$\bar{H}_{11}$	$\bar{H}_{11}$	$\bar{H}_{11}$	$\bar{H}_{12}$
σ_1	$\bar{H}_2$	$\bar{H}_2$	$\bar{H}_2$	$\bar{H}_2$

The semiautomata C_2 and D_2 are constructed:

C_2	$\bar{K}_1$	$\bar{K}_2$	$\bar{K}_3$
σ_0	$\bar{K}_1$	$\bar{K}_1$	$\bar{K}_1$
σ_1	$\bar{K}_2$	$\bar{K}_2$	$\bar{K}_2$

D_2	$\bar{L}_1$	$\bar{L}_2$
$(\bar{K}_1, \sigma_0)$	$\bar{L}_1$	$\bar{L}_1$
$(\bar{K}_1, \sigma_1)$	$\bar{L}_1$	$\bar{L}_1$
$(\bar{K}_2, \sigma_0)$	$\bar{L}_1$	$\bar{L}_1$
$(\bar{K}_2, \sigma_1)$	$\bar{L}_1$	$\bar{L}_1$
$(\bar{K}_3, \sigma_0)$	$\bar{L}_2$	$\bar{L}_2$
$(\bar{K}_3, \sigma_1)$	$\bar{L}_1$	$\bar{L}_1$

C_2 is isomorphic to F_1, D_2 is a two-state reset semiautomaton, and $C_2°D_2 \geq F_2$.

(c) $\pi'' = \{H_1 = \{123\}, H_2 = \{345\}, H_3 = \{5\}, H_4 = \{6\}\}$.

$F_2 = A/\pi''$	$\bar{H}_1$	$\bar{H}_2$	$\bar{H}_3$	$\bar{H}_4$
σ_0	$\bar{H}_1$	$\bar{H}_1$	$\bar{H}_1$	$\bar{H}_3$
σ_1	$\bar{H}_2$	$\bar{H}_2$	$\bar{H}_2$	$\bar{H}_2$

$\pi_m = \pi_2 = \{H_1 = \{123\}, H_2 = \{345\}\}$.

$\pi''' = \{H_3 = \{5\}, H_4 = \{6\}, H_{11} = \{1\}, H_{12} = \{2\}, H_{13} = \{3\}, H_{21} = \{4\},$

$\qquad H_{22} = \{3\}, H_{23} = \{5\}\}$.

The subsets of H_1 are ordered arbitrarily, those of H_2 according to Section 7.3 with $x_2 = \sigma_1$, $y_2 = \sigma_0$. Then

$$\sigma_1 \sigma_0 = \begin{pmatrix} 1 & 2 & 3 & 4 & 5 & 6 \\ 1 & 3 & 2 & 2 & 2 & 2 \end{pmatrix},$$

$(\sigma_1 \sigma_0)^2$ is the identity on H_1, and

$$\sigma_1 \sigma_0 \sigma_1 = \begin{pmatrix} 1 & 2 & 3 & 4 & 5 & 6 \\ 4 & 3 & 5 & 5 & 5 & 5 \end{pmatrix}$$

defines the order of the subsets of H_2.

	L_1	L_2	L_3
K_1	$\bar{H}_{11}$	$\bar{H}_{12}$	$\bar{H}_{13}$
K_2	$\bar{H}_{21}$	$\bar{H}_{22}$	$\bar{H}_{23}$
K_3	$\bar{H}_3$		
K_4	$\bar{H}_4$		

$A/\pi''' = F_3$	$\bar{H}_{11}$	$\bar{H}_{12}$	$\bar{H}_{13}$	$\bar{H}_{21}$	$\bar{H}_{22}$	$\bar{H}_{23}$	$\bar{H}_3$	$\bar{H}_4$
σ_0	$\bar{H}_{13}$	$\bar{H}_{11}$	$\bar{H}_{12}$	$\bar{H}_{11}$	$\bar{H}_{12}$	$\bar{H}_{13}$	$\bar{H}_{13}$	$\bar{H}_3$
σ_1	$\bar{H}_{21}$	$\bar{H}_{23}$	$\bar{H}_{22}$	$\bar{H}_{22}$	$\bar{H}_{22}$	$\bar{H}_{22}$	$\bar{H}_{22}$	$\bar{H}_{22}$

C_3	$\bar{K}_1$	$\bar{K}_2$	$\bar{K}_3$	$\bar{K}_4$
σ_0	$\bar{K}_1$	$\bar{K}_1$	$\bar{K}_1$	$\bar{K}_3$
σ_1	$\bar{K}_2$	$\bar{K}_2$	$\bar{K}_2$	$\bar{K}_2$

D_3	$\bar{L}_1$	$\bar{L}_2$	$\bar{L}_3$
$(\bar{K}_1, \sigma_0)$	$\bar{L}_3$	$\bar{L}_1$	$\bar{L}_2$
$(\bar{K}_1, \sigma_1)$	$\bar{L}_1$	$\bar{L}_3$	$\bar{L}_2$
$(\bar{K}_2, \sigma_0)$	$\bar{L}_1$	$\bar{L}_2$	$\bar{L}_3$
$(\bar{K}_2, \sigma_1)$	$\bar{L}_2$	$\bar{L}_2$	$\bar{L}_2$
$(\bar{K}_3, \sigma_0)$	$\bar{L}_3$	$\bar{L}_3$	$\bar{L}_3$
$(\bar{K}_3, \sigma_1)$	$\bar{L}_2$	$\bar{L}_2$	$\bar{L}_2$
$(\bar{K}_4, \sigma_0)$	$\bar{L}_1$	$\bar{L}_1$	$\bar{L}_1$
$(\bar{K}_4, \sigma_1)$	$\bar{L}_2$	$\bar{L}_2$	$\bar{L}_2$

C_3 is isomorphic to $A/\pi'' = F_2$, D_3 is a permutation-reset semiautomaton, and $C_3 \circ D_3 \geq F_3$.

The group generated by the permutation inputs $(\bar{K}_1, \sigma_0)$, $(\bar{K}_1, \sigma_1)$, and $(\bar{K}_2, \sigma_0)$ of D_3 is the symmetric group S_3 (the group of all permutations of three elements), and it is a homomorphic (actually an isomorphic) image of the subgroup of G_A composed of the elements:

$$\sigma_0^2 = \begin{pmatrix} 1 & 2 & 3 & 4 & 5 & 6 \\ 2 & 3 & 1 & 3 & 2 & 3 \end{pmatrix}, \quad \sigma_0^3 = \begin{pmatrix} 1 & 2 & 3 & 4 & 5 & 6 \\ 1 & 2 & 3 & 2 & 1 & 2 \end{pmatrix},$$

$$\sigma_0^4 = \begin{pmatrix} 1 & 2 & 3 & 4 & 5 & 6 \\ 3 & 1 & 2 & 1 & 3 & 1 \end{pmatrix},$$

$$\sigma_0^2 \sigma_1 \sigma_0 = \begin{pmatrix} 1 & 2 & 3 & 4 & 5 & 6 \\ 3 & 2 & 1 & 2 & 3 & 2 \end{pmatrix}, \quad \sigma_0^2 \sigma_1 \sigma_0^2 = \begin{pmatrix} 1 & 2 & 3 & 4 & 5 & 6 \\ 2 & 1 & 3 & 1 & 2 & 1 \end{pmatrix},$$

$$\sigma_0^2 \sigma_1 \sigma_0^3 = \begin{pmatrix} 1 & 2 & 3 & 4 & 5 & 6 \\ 1 & 3 & 2 & 3 & 1 & 3 \end{pmatrix}.$$

(d) All blocks in π''' are singletons and the construction is finished. F_3 covers A by the mapping

$$\eta = \begin{pmatrix} \bar{H}_{11} & \bar{H}_{12} & \bar{H}_{13} & \bar{H}_{21} & \bar{H}_{22} & \bar{H}_{23} & \bar{H}_3 & \bar{H}_4 \\ 1 & 2 & 3 & 4 & 3 & 5 & 5 & 6 \end{pmatrix}.$$

Indeed,

$$
\eta \sigma_0^A = \begin{pmatrix} \overline{H}_{11} & \overline{H}_{12} & \overline{H}_{13} & \overline{H}_{21} & \overline{H}_{22} & \overline{H}_{23} & \overline{H}_3 & \overline{H}_4 \\ 3 & 1 & 2 & 1 & 2 & 3 & 3 & 5 \end{pmatrix}
$$

$$
= \sigma_0^{F3} \eta
$$

$$
\eta \sigma_1^A = \begin{pmatrix} \overline{H}_{11} & \overline{H}_{12} & \overline{H}_{13} & \overline{H}_{21} & \overline{H}_{22} & \overline{H}_{23} & \overline{H}_3 & \overline{H}_4 \\ 4 & 5 & 3 & 3 & 3 & 3 & 3 & 3 \end{pmatrix}
$$

$$
= \sigma_1^{F3} \eta.
$$

But,

$$
A \le F_3 \le C_3 \,{}^\circ D_3 \simeq F_2 \,{}^\circ D_3 \le (C_2 \,{}^\circ D_2)\mathring{\omega}_1 D_3
$$

$$
\simeq (F_1 \,{}^\circ D_2)\mathring{\omega}_1 D_3 \le ((D_0 \,{}^\circ D_1)\mathring{\omega}_2 D_2)\mathring{\omega}_3 D_3.
$$

Here $D_0 = C_1$. The various mappings ω_i are defined as in Lemma B from Section 5.10.

D_0, D_1, D_2, D_3 are all permutation-reset semiautomata, and the groups generated by their permutation inputs are homomorphic images of subgroups of G_A. The methods of Chapter 6 can now be applied to obtain a covering of A by direct and cascade products of two-state reset semiautomata and simple grouplike semiautomata with simple groups, which are homomorphic images of subgroups of G_A.

7.9   The Necessity of Certain Components in a Cascade Product Covering of a Semiautomaton

It was proved in Chapter 6 that every semiautomaton can be covered by cascade and direct (which can be considered as particular cases of cascade) products of simple grouplike semiautomata and two-state reset semiautomata.

In Theorem A in Section 6.5, H need not be a normal subgroup of G; hence, one can cover a simple grouplike semiautomaton A in which G_A

has a nontrivial subgroup H by a cascade product $C \circ D$ of smaller semiautomata.

On the other hand, it will be shown in what follows that in the above case G_C or G_D must have a subgroup such that G_A is a homomorphic image of it; i.e., the obtained semiautomata have less states, but at least one of their semigroups is not less complicated than that of A. Because of this, only the simple grouplike and two-state reset semiautomata will be considered as *basic building blocks* (in what follows, used as a technical term) for cascade products covering a given semiautomaton.

A two-state reset semiautomaton is isomorphic (*after coinciding its equal inputs*) to one of the following five basic forms:

	σ_0			σ_0			σ_0	σ_1			σ_1	σ_2	$A2$	σ_0	σ_1	σ_2
s_1	s_1		s_1	s_1		s_1	s_1	s_1		s_1	s_1	s_2	s_1	s_1	s_1	s_2
s_2	s_1		s_2	s_2		s_2	s_2	s_1		s_2	s_1	s_2	s_2	s_2	s_1	s_2

The semigroups of these semiautomata are, respectively:

	σ_0			σ_0			σ_0	σ_1		$\wedge$	σ_1	σ_2		σ_0	σ_1	σ_2
σ_0	σ_0	σ_0	σ_0	σ_0	σ_0	σ_0	σ_1	$\wedge$	$\wedge$	σ_1	σ_2	σ_0	σ_0	σ_1	σ_2
						σ_1	σ_1	σ_1	σ_1	σ_1	σ_1	σ_2	σ_1	σ_1	σ_1	σ_2
							σ_2	σ_2	σ_1	σ_2	σ_2	σ_2	σ_2	σ_1	σ_2

$\wedge$ was introduced in the fourth case because G_A includes the identity by definition. In the other cases σ_0 is the identity. The first two semigroups are groups of order 1; a semigroup isomorphic to the third one will be denoted by R_1; the fourth and fifth semigroups are isomorphic and R will denote a semigroup isomorphic to them. All of the above two-state reset semiautomata can be covered by the fifth one, $A2$, and for uniqueness $A2$ will be referred to as the two-state reset semiautomaton in cascade product coverings using basic building blocks.

K. B. Krohn and J. L. Rhodes introduced the following definition:

DEFINITION.   A semigroup H is said to divide a semigroup G if H is a homomorphic image of a subsemigroup of G.

They also proved the following important theorem [22, 23]:

THEOREM.   (a) If a simple group H divides the semigroup G_A of a semiautomaton A, then in every covering of A by a cascade product (in particular, by a cascade product of basic building blocks) the semigroup of at least one of the factors is divisible by H.
          (b) If R or R_1 divides G_A, then in every covering of A by a cascade product of basic building blocks at least one factor is $A2$.

The proof of this theorem follows.

7.10   The Simple Group Case

THEOREM.   Let A, C, and D be semiautomata and assume that $C \overset{\circ}{\omega} D \geq A$. For every simple group H, which divides G_A, the semigroup G_C or G_D must be divisible by H.

Proof. $B = C \overset{\circ}{\omega} D \geq A \Rightarrow G_A$ is a homomorphic image of a subsemigroup of G_B (cf. Section 5.7). By the transitivity of homomorphism, H is also a homomorphic image of a subsemigroup of G_B, hence, by Theorem A in Section 1.16, of a subgroup K of G_B.
     The elements of G_B are mappings

$$x^B = \sigma_1^B \sigma_2^B \ldots \sigma_k^B \qquad (\sigma_i \in \Sigma^B = \Sigma^C)$$

of the set $S^C \times S^D$ into itself, defined as follows:

$$c \in S^C, d \in S^D : (c, d)x^B = (c, d)\sigma_1^B \sigma_2^B \ldots \sigma_k^B$$
$$= (c\sigma_1^C, d((c, \sigma_1)\omega)^D)\sigma_2^B \ldots \sigma_k^B$$
$$= (c\sigma_1^C \sigma_2^C, d((c, \sigma_1)\omega)^D((c\sigma_1^C, \sigma_2)\omega)^D)\sigma_3^B \ldots \sigma_k^B$$
$$= (cx^C, d((c, \sigma_1)\omega)^D \ldots ((c\sigma_1^C \ldots \sigma_{k-1}^C, \sigma_k)\omega)^D).$$

Notice that on the first component of a pair (c, d) the transformation x^B acts exactly as x^C in C.

By Theorem B in 1.16 there exists a subset W of $S^C \times S^D$ such that all transformations in K when restricted to W are permutations, and these permutations form a group isomorphic to K. Denote by W^C the projection of W on S^C, i.e., the set of all elements of S^C appearing in the pairs of W. Let K_1 consist of all $x^B \in K$ such that x^C is an identity on W^C. K_1 is not empty because the identity of K belongs to it. Moreover, K_1 is a subgroup of K, even a normal one, because for every $x^B \in K$

$$(x^B)^{-1} K_1 x^B \subseteq K_1.$$

x^B and y^B belong to the same coset of K_1 in K if and only if $x^B(y^B)^{-1} \in K_1$; hence, $x^C(y^C)^{-1}$, restricted to W^C, is the identity; i.e., x^C and y^C, when restricted to W^C, are equal permutations.

Thus, to each coset of K_1 in K there corresponds a distinct permutation of W^C, and the product of two such permutations corresponds to the product of the respective cosets in K/K_1. Hence, these permutations form a group isomorphic to K/K_1, and since they are restrictions of elements of G_C to a subset of S^C, K/K_1 is, by Theorem C in 1.16, a homomorphic image of a subgroup of G_C.

Now the group K_1 will be investigated. For $c \in W^C$ let $\{(c, d_1), (c, d_2), \ldots, (c, d_t)\}$ be the set of all pairs in W with c as the first component. Let $x^B = (\sigma_1 \sigma_2 \ldots \sigma_k)^B \in K_1$ and denote

$$((c, \sigma_1)\omega)^D ((c\sigma_1^C, \sigma_2)\omega)^D \ldots ((c\sigma_1^C \ldots \sigma_{k-1}^C, \sigma_k)\omega)^D = x_c^D.$$

x_c^D is an element of G_D.

x^B permutes the elements of W and, since $x^B \in K_1$ implies $cx^C = c$, x^B permutes the elements of the set $\{(c, d_1), \ldots, (c, d_t)\}$. But

$$(c, d_i)x^B = (cx^C, d_i x_c^D) = (c, d_i x_c^D).$$

Hence, x_c^D, when restricted to the set $\{d_1, d_2, \ldots, d_t\} \subseteq S^D$, permutes its elements.

The restrictions of the elements of K_1 to the set $\{(c, d_1), \ldots, (c, d_t)\}$ form a group K_c of permutations of this set, and it follows from the above that K_c is isomorphic to the group of permutations of $\{d_1, \ldots, d_t\}$ formed by the restrictions of the elements $\{x_c^D\}_{x^B \in K_1}$ of G_D to $\{d_1, \ldots, d_t\}$.

Hence, by Theorem C in 1.16, K_c is a homomorphic image of a subgroup of G_D. The same holds for every element of $W^C = \{c_1, c_2, \ldots, c_v\}$. W can be divided into v disjoint subsets

$$(c_1, d_{11}), (c_1, d_{12}), \ldots, (c_1, d_{1t_1})$$
$$(c_2, d_{21}), (c_2, d_{22}), \ldots, (c_2, d_{2t_2})$$
$$\vdots$$
$$(c_v, d_{v1}), (c_v, d_{v2}), \ldots, (c_v, d_{vt_v}),$$

and every $x^B \in K_1$, when restricted to W, permutes the pairs in every one of the above subsets independently. $K_{c_1}, K_{c_2}, \ldots, K_{c_v}$ are the corresponding groups of permutations of the subsets discussed above, and so the restriction of every $x^B \in K_1$ to W can be considered as an element of the direct product $K_{c_1} \times K_{c_2} \times \cdots \times K_{c_v}$. The restrictions of the elements of K_1 to W form a group isomorphic to K_1 (cf. Theorem B in 1.16); hence, K_1 is isomorphic to a subgroup of the direct product $K_{c_1} \times K_{c_2} \times \cdots \times K_{c_v}$.

To finish the proof notice that by Lemma B in Section 1.15 the simple group H, being a homomorphic image of K, must be a homomorphic image of K/K_1 or of K_1. In the first case it divides G_C because K/K_1 divides G_C. In the second case, by Lemma D in 1.15, which, clearly, can be expanded to any finite number of factors, H divides one of the K_{c_i}'s, and since every K_{c_i} is a homomorphic image of a subgroup of G_D, H divides G_D.

Assume that A is covered by a cascade product of n semiautomata $A_1, \ldots, A_n$, i.e.,

$$A \leq ((\ldots(A_1 \mathring{\omega}_1 A_2)\mathring{\omega}_2 \ldots)\mathring{\omega}_{n-2} A_{n-1})\mathring{\omega}_{n-1} A_n.$$

If a simple group H divides G_A, then, by the theorem, H necessarily divides G_{A_n} or G_E, where

$$E = (\ldots(A_1 \mathring{\omega}_1 A_2)\mathring{\omega}_2 \ldots)\mathring{\omega}_{n-2} A_{n-1}.$$

In the last case H necessarily divides $G_{A_{n-1}}$ or G_F, where

$$F = (\ldots(A_1 \mathring{\omega}_1 A_2)\mathring{\omega}_2 \ldots)\mathring{\omega}_{n-3} A_{n-2},$$

and so on. Part (a) of the theorem in 7.9 is thus proved.

A simple nontrivial H cannot divide the semigroup R of a two-state reset semiautomaton appearing as a basic building block in a cascade product covering of a semiautomaton A. Thus, if H divides G_A it must divide some G_B, where B is a simple grouplike semiautomaton in the above covering. Such a G_B is a simple group, but it may have proper subgroups divisible by H. So it is possible that among the basic building blocks, one having the structure of H will not appear. However, suppose that in the set $\{H_1, H_2, \ldots, H_r\}$ of all simple groups which divide G_A, say, H_1 does not divide any of the other groups in this set (this is true, for example, if all these groups are Abelian, hence, cyclic groups of prime order). In every covering of A by a cascade product of basic building blocks in which the simple grouplike components have only groups which divide G_A, there exists at least one simple grouplike semiautomaton B having the structure of H_1.

7.11   The Reset Case

LEMMA.   If the semigroup R from Section 7.9 is a homomorphic image of a finite semigroup T, then T has a subsemigroup isomorphic to R.

Proof.   Let φ be the homomorphism of T onto R. $\sigma_0\varphi^{-1}$ is a subsemigroup of T, and by finiteness there necessarily exists an idempotent e in it. $T_1 = eTe$ is a subsemigroup of T with e as a two-sided identity, and the restriction φ_1 of φ to T_1 is a homomorphism of T_1 *onto* R because

$$T_1\varphi_1 = T_1\varphi = (eTe)\varphi = (e\varphi)(T\varphi)(e\varphi) = \sigma_0 R\sigma_0 = R.$$

The elements $\{\sigma_1, \sigma_2\}$ form a subsemigroup of R; hence, $T_2 = \sigma_1\varphi_1^{-1} \cup \sigma_2\varphi_1^{-1}$ is a subsemigroup of T_1. Let T_3 be a minimal subsemigroup of T_2 such that $T_3\varphi_1 = \{\sigma_1, \sigma_2\}$. For any $x \in T_3$, the set xT_3 is a subsemigroup of T_3 $[xt_3' \cdot xt_3'' = x(t_3'xt_3'') \in xT_3]$, and, since

$$(xT_3)\varphi_1 = x\varphi_1 \cdot T_3\varphi_1 = x\varphi_1 \cdot \{\sigma_1, \sigma_2\} = \{\sigma_1, \sigma_2\},$$

the minimality of T_3 implies $xT_3 = T_3$.

Now, $\sigma_1\varphi_1^{-1} \cap T_3$ and $\sigma_2\varphi_1^{-1} \cap T_3$ are nonempty disjoint subsemigroups of T_3, and each has an idempotent, say, y and z, respectively. But

$$yT_3 = T_3 \Rightarrow \exists\, u \in T_3,\ yu = z \Rightarrow yz = yyu = yu = z.$$

Similarly, $zy = y$, and since e is a two-sided identity for y and z, the triple $\{e, y, z\}$ forms a subsemigroup of T_1, hence also of T, isomorphic to R.

REMARK.   This lemma also holds when R is replaced by R_1. In this case, like above, T_1 and φ_1 exist such that $T_1\varphi_1 = R_1$. One proceeds:

The element σ_1 forms a subsemigroup of R_1; hence, $T_2 = \sigma_1\varphi_1^{-1}$ is a subsemigroup of T_1. There exists an idempotent $y \in T_2$ and since e is a two-sided identity for y, the pair $\{e, y\}$ forms a subsemigroup of T_1, hence also of T, isomorphic to R_1.

THEOREM.   Let A, C, and D be semiautomata and assume that $C \mathring{\omega} D \geq A$. If the semigroup R divides G_A, then G_C or G_D must be divisible by R.

Proof. $B = C \mathring{\omega} D \geq A \Rightarrow G_A$ is a homomorphic image of a subsemigroup of G_B. Hence, R is also a homomorphic image of a subsemigroup of G_B. By the lemma there exist in this subsemigroup, hence, in G_B, three elements, z^B, x^B, y^B, which form a semigroup isomorphic to R. If z^B is the two-sided identity in this semigroup, then $\{1, x^B, y^B\}$ also form a semigroup isomorphic to R (1 is the identity of G_B).

$$x^B \neq y^B \Rightarrow \exists\, (c, d) \in S^B$$

such that

$$(c_1, d_1) = (c, d)x^B \neq (c, d)y^B = (c_2, d_2).$$

Now

$$x^Bx^B = x^B, \qquad x^By^B = y^B, \qquad y^Bx^B = x^B, \qquad y^By^B = y^B$$

imply:

$$(c_1, d_1)x^B = (c, d)x^B x^B = (c, d)x^B = (c_1, d_1)$$
$$(c_1, d_1)y^B = (c, d)x^B y^B = (c, d)y^B = (c_2, d_2)$$
$$(c_2, d_2)x^B = (c, d)y^B x^B = (c, d)x^B = (c_1, d_1)$$
$$(c_2, d_2)y^B = (c, d)y^B y^B = (c, d)y^B = (c_2, d_2).$$

If $c_1 \neq c_2$, then $c_1 x^C = c_1$, $c_1 y^C = c_2$, imply $x^C \neq y^C$, and the set $\{1, x^C, y^C\} \subseteq G_C$ forms a subsemigroup isomorphic to R. (Notice that $x^B y^B = y^B \Rightarrow x^C y^C = y^C$, etc.)

If $c_1 = c_2$, then necessarily $d_1 \neq d_2$. Using the notation x_c^D introduced in Section 7.10 one obtains:

$$(c_1, d_1) = (c_1, d_1)x^B = (c_1 x^C, d_1 x_{c_1}^D),$$

that is,

$$d_1 x_{c_1}^D = d_1.$$

Similarly:

$$(c_1, d_1)y^B = (c_1, d_2) \Rightarrow d_1 y_{c_1}^D = d_2$$
$$(c_1, d_2)x^B = (c_1, d_1) \Rightarrow d_2 x_{c_1}^D = d_1$$
$$(c_1, d_2)y^B = (c_1; d_2) \Rightarrow d_2 y_{c_1}^D = d_2.$$

Consequently, the restrictions of the identity and of the mappings $x_{c_1}^D$ and $y_{c_1}^D$ of G_D to the elements $d_1, d_2 \in S^D$ are

$$\begin{pmatrix} d_1 & d_2 \\ d_1 & d_2 \end{pmatrix}, \quad \begin{pmatrix} d_1 & d_2 \\ d_1 & d_1 \end{pmatrix}, \quad \begin{pmatrix} d_1 & d_2 \\ d_2 & d_2 \end{pmatrix},$$

respectively. These three mappings form a semigroup isomorphic to R. On the other hand, this semigroup is a homomorphic image of the sub-semigroup of G_D generated by the identity, $x_{c_1}^D$, and $y_{c_1}^D$. Thus, the theorem also holds in the case $c_1 = c_2$.

REMARK.   The theorem also holds when R is replaced by R_1.
Indeed, let $\{1, x^B\}$ form a subsemigroup of G^B isomorphic to R_1 (it exists by the previous remark).

$$x^B \neq 1 \Rightarrow \exists\, (c, d) \in S^B$$

such that

$$(c, d)x^B = (c_1, d_1) \neq (c, d).$$

$$(c_1, d_1)x^B = (c, d)x^B x^B = (c, d)x^B = (c_1, d_1),$$

because $x^B x^B = x^B$.

If $c_1 \neq c$, then $1_{G_C} \neq x^C$ ($c1_{G_C} = c$, but $cx^C = c_1$) and $\{1_{G_C}, x^C\}$ is a subsemigroup of G_C isomorphic to R_1.

If $c_1 = c$, then necessarily $d_1 \neq d$.

$$(c_1, d_1) = (c_1, d_1)x^B = (c_1 x^C, d_1 x^D_{c_1}),$$

that is,

$$d_1 x^D_{c_1} = d_1.$$

Consequently, the restrictions of the identity and of $x^D_{c_1}$ in G_D to the elements $d, d_1 \in S^D$ are

$$\begin{pmatrix} d & d_1 \\ d & d_1 \end{pmatrix} \quad \text{and} \quad \begin{pmatrix} d & d_1 \\ d_1 & d_1 \end{pmatrix},$$

respectively. These two mappings form a semigroup isomorphic to R_1, and the conclusion follows as before.

Part (b) of the theorem in Section 7.9 can now be obtained by the same reasoning as in 7.10, using the theorem in the present section, and using the fact that neither R nor R_1 can be a homomorphic image of a group.

7.12   Group Free Regular Sets†

The developed algebraic theory may be used to prove the equivalence of two special families of regular sets: the *noncounting* and *star free* regular sets. It is particularly interesting that although neither of these families is defined in terms of semigroups, as far as the author knows all existing proofs of their equivalence appeal strongly to the theory of semigroups.

DEFINITION.   A regular set $U \subseteq \Sigma^*$ is a *noncounting regular set* if and only if there is an integer $k_u \geq 0$ such that for every $w_1, y, w_2 \in \Sigma^*$

$$w_1 y^{k_u} w_2 \in U \Leftrightarrow w_1 y^{k_u + 1} w_2 \in U.$$

Noncounting regular sets are so designated because an automaton accepting such a set need never count (modulo any integer greater than one) the number of consecutive occurrences of any subword when the number of such occurrences exceeds a certain bound. Indeed, it follows from the definition that $w_1 y^{k_u} w_2 \in U \Rightarrow w_1 y^p w_2 \in U$ for any integer $p \geq k_u$.

DEFINITION.   A set $U \subseteq \Sigma^*$ is a *star free set* if and only if it is obtainable from the letters of Σ (considered as singletons) by a finite number of applications of the operations $+$, $\cdot$, $\cap$ and $'$ $(T' = \Sigma^* - T)$.

The following theorem is due to Schützenberger [41]. The proof given here was developed by A. Meyer following a paper by Papert and McNaughton [32].

THEOREM.   A set $U \subseteq \Sigma^*$ is a star free set if and only if it is a noncounting regular set.

Proof.   To show that a star free set is a noncounting regular set notice first that the letters of Σ (considered as singletons) are regular

---

† This section is written by Professor Albert R. Meyer from Carnegie–Mellon University, Pittsburgh, Pennsylvania.

sets, and since regular sets are closed under $+$, $\cdot$, $\cap$ and $'$ every star free set is a regular one. Now the letters of Σ are trivially noncounting regular sets (choose $k_{\{\sigma\}} = 2$). Thus, it is sufficient to show that if U and V are noncounting regular sets, then so are UV, $U + V$, $U \cap V$, and U'. This will be done for UV; the remaining cases follow more easily.

Let U, V be noncounting regular sets. Denote $k = k_u + k_v + 1$, and suppose that $w_1 y^k w_2 \in UV$ for some $w_1, y, w_2 \in \Sigma^*$. There are words $u \in U$ and $v \in V$ such that $uv = w_1 y^k w_2 = w_1 y^{k_u} y y^{k_v} w_2$. Hence either $u = w_1 y^{k_u} t_1$ for some $t_1 \in \Sigma^*$ or $u = t_2 y^{k_v} w_2$ for some $t_2 \in \Sigma^*$. But

$$u = w_1 y^{k_u} t_1 \in U \Rightarrow w_1 y^{k_u + 1} t_1 \in U$$

and similarly

$$v = t_2 y^{k_v} w_2 \in V \Rightarrow t_2 y^{k_v + 1} w_2 \in V.$$

In either case if follows that

$$w_1 y^{k_u + k_v + 2} w_2 = w_1 y^{k + 1} w_2 \in UV.$$

The same argument may be reversed to show that

$$w_1 y^{k + 1} w_2 = w_1 y^{k_u} y y y^{k_v} w_2 \in UV \Rightarrow w_1 y^{k_u} y y^{k_v} w_2$$
$$= w_1 y^k w_2 \in UV,$$

i.e., UV is noncounting.

The proof in the other direction is much harder. One starts with a definition.

DEFINITION.   For any set $U \subseteq \Sigma^*$, E_u will denote the following relation over E^*:

$$x E_u y \Leftrightarrow (w_1 x w_2 \in U \Leftrightarrow w_1 y w_2 \in U \quad \text{for all} \quad w_1, w_2 \in \Sigma^*).$$

The argument of Section 3.4 may be repeated to show that E_u is a congruence on Σ^*, and U is a union of complete congruence classes of E_u.

Comparison of the definitions of E_u and of a noncounting regular set shows that U is such a set if and only if there is a $k_u \geq 0$ such that $y^{k_u} E_u y^{k_u + 1}$ for all $y \in \Sigma^*$.

One more definition is needed.

DEFINITION.   A semiautomaton A will be called *group free* if and only if its semigroup G_A has no divisor which is a nontrivial group. A regular set U is a *group free regular set* if and only if there is an automaton $\hat{A}$ accepting U such that the semiautomaton A of $\hat{A}$ is group free.

LEMMA A.   Every noncounting regular set is a group free regular set.

Proof.   Any regular set U is a union of congruence classes of some congruence E on Σ^* such that the index of E is finite (Theorem Λ in 3.2). For all $w_1, w_2 \in \Sigma^*$,

$$x \, E \, y \Rightarrow w_1 x w_2 \, E \, w_1 y w_2 \Rightarrow (w_1 x w_2 \in U \Leftrightarrow w_1 y w_2 \subset U),$$

i.e., $E \subseteq E_u$ and since E is of finite index so is E_u. The automaton $\hat{A}$ constructed from E_u (by the method in 3.2) accepts U and by construction

$$x^A = y^A \Leftrightarrow x E_u y \qquad \text{for} \quad x, y \in \Sigma^*.$$

Now, if U is a noncounting regular set,

$$y^{k_u} E_u y^{k_u + 1} \Rightarrow (y^A)^{k_u} = (y^A)^{k_u + 1} \qquad \text{for every} \quad y \in \Sigma^*.$$

If G_A has some nontrivial group as a divisor, then it has some nontrivial subgroup (Theorem A in 1.16), and, for any element y^A in this subgroup such that y^A is not the identity of the subgroup, $(y^A)^n \neq (y^A)^{n+1}$ for any $n \geq 0$. Hence, G_A has no nontrivial group divisors, and U is a group free regular set, which proves the lemma.

Let now U be a group free regular set and $\hat{A}$ an automaton accepting it, with a group free semiautomaton A. The main theorem in 7.1 implies that every group free semiautomaton can be covered by a cascade product of two-state reset semiautomata. Let B be such a cascade product covering A. Given B, one can find another cascade product C of two-state reset semiautomata such that $C \geq A$ and $\Sigma^C = \Sigma^A$. The theorem in Section 5.6 (which applies to Rabin–Scott automata in an obvious way) implies that there is an automaton $\hat{C}$ with semiautomaton C which also accepts U. Thus, the following lemma holds:

LEMMA B.　　Every group free regular set can be accepted by some automaton whose semiautomaton is a cascade product of two-state reset semiautomata. The proof of the theorem is completed by

LEMMA C.　　If $U \subseteq \Sigma^*$ is accepted by some automaton $\hat{A}$ such that the semiautomaton A of $\hat{A}$ is a cascade product of two-state reset semiautomata, then U is a star free regular set.

Proof.　Let C be a two-state reset semiautomaton, $S^C = \{1, 2\}$, $\Sigma^C = \Sigma_1 \cup \Sigma_2 \cup \Sigma_I$, where Σ_1, Σ_2, and Σ_I are the reset to 1, reset to 2 and identity inputs, respectively. For $s, t \in S^C$ let $R_{st}^C = \{x \in \Sigma^* | sx^C = t\}$.

Any $x \in R_{12}^C$ must equal $y\sigma_2 z$ for some $y \in (\Sigma^C)^*$, $\sigma_2 \in \Sigma_2$, and $z \in (\Sigma^C)^*$. Moreover, z may be chosen so that no $\sigma_1 \in \Sigma_1$ occurs in it, i.e., $z \notin (\Sigma^C)^* \sigma_1 (\Sigma^C)^*$. Conversely, every such $y\sigma_2 z$ is in R_{12}^C, i.e.,

$$R_{12}^C = (\Sigma^C)^* \Sigma^2 ((\Sigma^C)^* \Sigma_1 (\Sigma^C)^*)'.$$

But $\phi = \{\sigma\} \cap \{\sigma\sigma\}$ for any $\sigma \in \Sigma^C$, and $(\Sigma^C)^* = \phi'$. Hence $(\Sigma^C)^*$ and consequently also R_{12}^C are star free sets. So is also R_{11}^C, because $R_{11}^C = (R_{12}^C)'$. Repeating the argument with the roles of 1 and 2 reversed, it follows that R_{st}^C is a star free regular set for any $s, t \in S^C$.

Proceeding by induction, let B be a semiautomaton which is a cascade product of n two-state reset semiautomata and assume that R_{st}^B is a star free regular set for any $s, t \in S^B$.

Let $D = B \tilde{\omega} C$ and consider $x \in R_{(s,1)(t,2)}^D$. Then $x \in R_{st}^B$ but also $x = y\sigma z$ for some $y \in R_{sr}^B$ and $r \in S^B$ such that $(r, \sigma)\omega \in \Sigma_2$, and some $z \in (\Sigma^B)^* = (\Sigma^D)^*$. Choose a z such that no prefix $w\delta$ of z can change back the state of C, i.e., $(r\sigma^B w^B, \delta)\omega \notin \Sigma_1$, or what is the same thing, $z \notin (\cup R^B_{r\sigma^B,q}\delta)(\Sigma^B)^*$ the union being over all $q \in S^B$, $\delta \in \Sigma^B$ such that $(q, \delta)\omega \in \Sigma_1$. Conversely, every such $y\sigma z$ in R^B_{st} is also in $R^D_{(s,1)(t,2)}$ and altogether one has

$$R^D_{(s,1)(t,2)} = R^B_{st} \cap [\cup R^B_{sr}\sigma(\cup R^B_{r\sigma^B,q}\delta(\Sigma^B)^*)']$$

the left-hand union being over all $r \in S^B$, $\sigma \in \Sigma^B$ such that $(r, \sigma)\omega \in \Sigma_2$, and the right-hand union being over all $q \in S^B$, $\delta \in \Sigma^B$ such that $(q, \delta)\omega \in \Sigma_1$. These are finite unions, and so $R^D_{(s,1)(t,2)}$ is a star free regular set as is

$$R^D_{(s,1)(t,1)} = R^B_{st} \cap (R^D_{(s,1)(t,2)})'.$$

Again repeating the argument with 1 and 2 reversed, it follows that R^D_{ab} for any a, $b \in S^D$ is a star free regular set.

By induction, a semiautomaton A which is a cascade product of two-state reset semiautomata has R^A_{ab} a star free regular set for any a, $b \in S^A$. If $\hat{A}$ accepts U and s^A_0 is the initial state, then $U = \bigcup_{b \in F^A} R_{s^A_0 b}$, hence U is a star free regular set.

7.13   Concluding Remarks

The theorem in Section 7.1 shows that for a given semiautomaton A, simple grouplike semiautomata with groups dividing G_A and two-state reset semiautomata are sufficient to construct a cascade product covering of A. If only these semiautomata are considered, as basic building blocks for cascade product coverings of the above A, then the theorem in 7.9 provides information about the necessity of some of them. The following two examples indicate cases where this information is not complete.

(i)   The simple grouplike semiautomaton A with the group A_5 (the group of all even permutations of five elements) is covered by one basic building block of the above kind, A itself. There are nontrivial simple groups dividing A_5 which are not represented by corresponding simple grouplike semiautomata in the above covering.

(ii)   The semigroup G_A of the two-state reset semiautomaton

A	σ_0
s_1	s_1
s_2	s_2

is the one-element group G_1, and the only semigroups dividing it are G_1 again. Nevertheless, it is impossible to construct a cascade product of grouplike semiautomata having the structure of G_1 such that it will cover A. Indeed, every cascade product of one-state semiautomata has one state, and it cannot be mapped onto the two states in S^A.

One can cover A using the two-state reset semiautomaton $A2$, although neither R nor R_1 divides G_A. The simple grouplike semiautomaton with the simple group Z_2 of order two covers A also, but it is excluded because Z_2 does not divide G_A.

Finally, notice that the above theory does not indicate how many of any particular basic building blocks are needed to construct a cascade product covering of a given semiautomaton.

The reader will find further results and developments of the decomposition theory in [20, 21, 25].

Bibliography

1. Aanderaa, S., On the algebra of regular expressions, *Appl. Math.* Harvard University, Cambridge, Massachusetts, 1–18 (1965), (ditto).

2. Arden, D. N., Delayed logic and finite state machines. *Theory of Computing Machine Design*, pp. 1–35. Univ. of Michigan Press, Ann Arbor, Michigan, 1960.

3. Birkhoff, G., "Lattice Theory," Vol. XXV of *Amer. Math. Soc. Colloquium Publications*. Amer. Math. Soc., Providence, Rhode Island, 1948.

4. Brzozowski, J. A., Canonical regular expressions and minimal state graphs for definite events. *Proc. Symp. Math. Theory of Automata, Brooklyn, N. Y., 1962* pp. 529–561. Wiley, New York, 1963.

5. Brzozowski, J. A., Derivatives of regular expressions. *J. ACM* **11**, 481–494 (1964).

6. Clifford, A. H. and G. R. Preston, "The Algebraic Theory of Semigroups," Vol. 1. *Math Surveys No. 7*. Amer. Math. Soc., Providence, Rhode Island, 1962.

7. Cohen, R., Cascade decomposition of automata (in Hebrew). Master thesis; Technion, Israel Institute of Technology, Haifa, Israel, 1966.

8. Eggan, L. C., Transition graphs and the star-height of regular events. *Michigan Math. J.* **10**, 385–397 (1963).

9. Ghiron, H., Rules to manipulate regular expressions of finite automata. *IRE Trans.* **EC-11**, 574–575 (1962).

10. Ginsburg, S., "An Introduction to Mathematical Machine Theory." Addison-Wesley, Reading, Massachusetts, 1962.

11. Ginzburg, A., A procedure for checking equality of regular expressions. *J. ACM* **14**, 355–362 (1967).

12. Ginzburg, A. and M. Yoeli, Products of automata and the problem of covering. *Trans. Amer. Math. Soc.* **116**, 253–266 (1965).

13. Glushkov, V. M., The abstract theory of automata (in Russian). *Usp. Mat. Nauk.* **16**, No. 5, 3–62 (1961).

14. Hall, M., Jr., "The Theory of Groups." Macmillan, New York, 1959.

15. Harrison, M. A., "Introduction to Switching and Automata Theory." McGraw-Hill, New York, 1965.

16. Hartmanis, J., Loop-free structure of sequential machines. *Information and Control* **5**, 25–43 (1962).

17. Hartmanis, J. and R. E. Stearns, Some dangers in state reduction of sequential machines. *Information and Control* **5**, 252–260 (1962).

18. Hartmanis, J. and R. E. Stearns, "Algebraic Structure Theory of Sequential Machines." Prentice-Hall, Englewood Cliffs, New Jersey, 1966.

19. Kleene, S. C., Representation of events in nerve nets and finite automata. *In* "Automata Studies," pp. 3–41. Princeton Univ. Press, Princeton, New Jersey, 1956.

20. Krohn, K. B., R. Mateosian, and J. L. Rhodes, Complexity of ideals in finite semigroups and finite-state machines. *Math. Systems Theory* **1**, 59–66 (1967).

21. Krohn, K. B., R. Mateosian, and J. L. Rhodes, Methods of the algebraic theory of machines. I. Decomposition theorem for generalized machines; Properties preserved under series and parallel compositions of machines. *J. Computer and Systems Sci.* **1**, 55–85 (1967).

22. Krohn, K. B. and J. L. Rhodes, Algebraic theory of machines. *Proc. Symp. Math. Theory of Automata, Brooklyn, N.Y., 1962* pp. 341–384. Wiley, New York, 1963.

23. Krohn, K. B. and J. L. Rhodes, Algebraic theory of machines. I. Prime decomposition theorem for finite semigroups and machines. *Trans. Amer. Math. Soc.* **116**, 450–464 (1965).

24. Krohn, K. B. and J. L. Rhodes, Results on finite semigroups derived from the algebraic theory of machines. *Proc. Natl. Acad. Sci. U.S.*, **53**, 499–501 (1965).

25. Krohn, K. B. and J. L. Rhodes, Complexity of finite semigroups and finite-state machines, The general case. To appear in *Proc. Conf. Algebraic Theory of Machines, Languages and Semigroups, Asilomar, Pacific Grove, California, 1966.*

26. Kurosh, A., "The Theory of Groups." Chelsea Publ. Co., New York, 1955.

27. McNaughton, R., Techniques for manipulating regular expressions. Machines Structures Group Memo No. 10, pp. 1–27. MIT Project MAC, Cambridge, Massachusetts, Nov. 1965.

28. McNaughton, R. and H. Yamada, Regular expressions and state graphs for automata. *Trans. IRE* **EC-9**, 39–47 (1960).

29. Mealy, G. H., A method for synthesizing sequential circuits. *Bell System Tech. J.* **34**, 1045–1079 (1955).

30. Moore, E. F., Gedanken—experiments on sequential machines. *In* "Automata Studies," pp. 129–153. Princeton Univ. Press, Princeton, New Jersey, 1956.

31. Nerode, A., Linear automaton transformations. *Proc. Amer. Math. Soc.* **9**, 541–544 (1958).

32. Papert, S. and R. McNaughton, The fundamentals of the algebraic theory of machines, and the monoid characterization of non-counting events. Project MAC, MIT, July 1966, (ditto).

33. Paull, M. C. and S. H. Unger, Minimizing the number of states in incompletely specified sequential switching functions. *IRE Trans.* **EC-8**, 356–367 (1959).

34. Paz, A. and B. Peleg, Ultimate-definite and symmetric-definite events and automata. *J. ACM* **12**, 399–410 (1965).

35. Perles, M., M. O. Rabin, and E. Shamir, The theory of definite automata *IEEE Trans. Electron. Computers* **EC–12**, 233–243 (1963).

36. Polytechnic Institute of Brooklyn, Mathematical theory of automata. *Proc. Symp. Math. Theory of Automata, Brooklyn, N.Y., 1962.* Wiley, New York, 1963.

37. Rabin, M. O. and D. Scott, Finite automata and their decision problems. *IBM J. Res. Develop.* **3**, 114–125 (1959).

38. Redko, V. N., On defining relations for the algebra of regular events (in Russian). *Ukrain. Mat. Z.* **16**, 120–126 (1964).

39. Rhodes, J. L., Some results on finite semigroups. *J. Algebra* **4**, 471–504 (1966).

40. Salomaa, A. Two complete axiom systems for the algebra of regular events. *J. ACM* **13**, 158–169 (1966).

41. Schützenberger, M. P., On finite monoids having only trivial subgroups. *Information and Control* **8**, 190–194 (1965).

42. Yoeli, M., The cascade decomposition of sequential machines. *IRE Trans.* **EC-10**, 587–592 (1961).

43. Yoeli, M., Cascade-parallel decompositions of sequential machines. *IRE Trans.* **EC-12**, 322–324 (1963).

44. Yoeli, M., Decomposition of finite automata. Tech. Rept. No. 10, U.S. Office of Naval Research, Information Systems Branch, Hebrew University, Jerusalem, Israel, 1963.

45. Yoeli, M., Canonical representation of chain events. *Information and Control* **8**, 180–189 (1965).

46. Yoeli, M., Generalized cascade decompositions of automata. *J. ACM* **12**, 411–422 (1965).

47. Yoeli, M. and A. Ginzburg, On homomorphic images of transition graphs. *J. Franklin Inst.* **278**, 291–296 (1964).

48. Zeiger, H. P., Loop-free synthesis of finite state machines. Ph.D. Thesis Elec. Eng. Department, M.I.T., 1964.

49. Zeiger, H. P., Cascade synthesis of finite-state machines. *Information and Control* **10**, 419–433 (1967).

50. Zeiger, H. P., Yet another proof of the cascade decomposition theorem for finite automata. *Math. Systems Theory* **1**, 225–228 (1967).

Index